T0192351

Communications
in Computer and Information Science   1975

Rationale

The CCIS series is devoted to the publication of proceedings of computer science conferences. Its aim is to efficiently disseminate original research results in informatics in printed and electronic form. While the focus is on publication of peer-reviewed full papers presenting mature work, inclusion of reviewed short papers reporting on work in progress is welcome, too. Besides globally relevant meetings with internationally representative program committees guaranteeing a strict peer-reviewing and paper selection process, conferences run by societies or of high regional or national relevance are also considered for publication.

Topics

The topical scope of CCIS spans the entire spectrum of informatics ranging from foundational topics in the theory of computing to information and communications science and technology and a broad variety of interdisciplinary application fields.

Information for Volume Editors and Authors

Publication in CCIS is free of charge. No royalties are paid, however, we offer registered conference participants temporary free access to the online version of the conference proceedings on SpringerLink (http://link.springer.com) by means of an http referrer from the conference website and/or a number of complimentary printed copies, as specified in the official acceptance email of the event.

CCIS proceedings can be published in time for distribution at conferences or as post-proceedings, and delivered in the form of printed books and/or electronically as USBs and/or e-content licenses for accessing proceedings at SpringerLink. Furthermore, CCIS proceedings are included in the CCIS electronic book series hosted in the SpringerLink digital library at http://link.springer.com/bookseries/7899. Conferences publishing in CCIS are allowed to use Online Conference Service (OCS) for managing the whole proceedings lifecycle (from submission and reviewing to preparing for publication) free of charge.

Publication process

The language of publication is exclusively English. Authors publishing in CCIS have to sign the Springer CCIS copyright transfer form, however, they are free to use their material published in CCIS for substantially changed, more elaborate subsequent publications elsewhere. For the preparation of the camera-ready papers/files, authors have to strictly adhere to the Springer CCIS Authors' Instructions and are strongly encouraged to use the CCIS LaTeX style files or templates.

Abstracting/Indexing

CCIS is abstracted/indexed in DBLP, Google Scholar, EI-Compendex, Mathematical Reviews, SCImago, Scopus. CCIS volumes are also submitted for the inclusion in ISI Proceedings.

How to start

To start the evaluation of your proposal for inclusion in the CCIS series, please send an e-mail to ccis@springer.com.

Naipeng Dong · Babu Pillai · Guangdong Bai · Mark Utting

Editors

Distributed Ledger Technology

7th International Symposium, SDLT 2023
Brisbane, QLD, Australia, November 30 – December 1, 2023
Revised Selected Papers

 Springer

Editors
Naipeng Dong [ID]
University of Queensland
Brisbane, QLD, Australia

Babu Pillai [ID]
Southern Cross University
Bilinga, QLD, Australia

Guangdong Bai [ID]
University of Queensland
Brisbane, QLD, Australia

Mark Utting [ID]
University of Queensland
Brisbane, QLD, Australia

ISSN 1865-0929   ISSN 1865-0937 (electronic)
Communications in Computer and Information Science
ISBN 978-981-97-0005-9   ISBN 978-981-97-0006-6 (eBook)
https://doi.org/10.1007/978-981-97-0006-6

This Springer imprint is published by the registered company Springer Nature Singapore Pte Ltd.
The registered company address is: 152 Beach Road, #21-01/04 Gateway East, Singapore 189721, Singapore

Paper in this product is recyclable.

Preface

The Symposium on Distributed Ledger Technology (SDLT) is an international conference for both research and industry in all areas related to the emerging distributed ledger technology. DLT provides a way to store and manage information in a distributed fashion, and thus enables the creation of decentralized crypto-currencies, smart contracts, eGovernance, supply chain management, eVoting, etc over a network of computer systems without any human intervention. Unprecedented reliability and security over other cryptographic schemes has expanded the application domains of blockchain including financial services, real estate, stock exchange, identity management, supply chain, and Internet of Things. Since 2017, SDLT has served as a forum for researchers, business leaders and policy makers in this area to carefully analyse current systems or propose new solutions creating a scientific background for a solid development of innovative Distributed Ledger Technology applications. The previous 6 events were hosted in Gold Coast (1st 2017, 2nd 2018, 3rd 2018, and 6th 2022) and in Brisbane (4th 2019 and 5th 2021), Australia.

This 7th SDLT took place in The University of Queensland, Brisbane, Australia on 31 November – 1 December 2023. The Program committee (PC) received 32 research papers from both academia and industry. The review process went through two stages. The first stage filtered out 7 papers that were not in the scope or in the correct format. In this stage, each submission was reviewed by two program co-chairs in single-blind manner. For the remaining 25 papers, each submission was reviewed by at least 3 Program Committee members in double-blind manner. The committee decided to accept 8 full papers and 1 short paper.

November 2023

Naipeng Dong
Babu Pillai

Organization

General Chairs

Mark Utting   University of Queensland, Australia
Guangdong Bai   University of Queensland, Australia

Program Committee Chairs

Naipeng Dong   University of Queensland, Australia
Babu Pillai   Southern Cross University, Australia

Program Committee

Abigail Koay	University of the Sunshine Coast, Australia
Babu Pillai	Southern Cross University, Australia
David Hyland-Wood	Griffith University, Australia
David Pearce	ConsenSys, New Zealand
Dileepa Fernando	Nanyang Technological University, Singapore
Dorottya Zelenyanszki	Griffith University, Australia
Ed Young	Crystal Delta, Australia
Ermyas Abebe	ConsenSys, Australia
Guangdong Bai	University of Queensland, Australia
Golam Sorwar	Southern Cross University, Australia
Gowri Ramachandran	Queensland University of Technology, Australia
Jubilant Job	Southern Cross University, Australia
Jubilant Kizhakkethottam	Saintgits College of Engineering, India
Joanne Fuller	ConsenSys, Australia
Kamanashis Biswas	Australian Catholic University, Australia
Katrina Donaghy	Civic Ledger, Australia
Kulani Mahadewa	National University of Singapore, Singapore
Marius Portmann	University of Queensland, Australia
Mark Utting	University of Queensland, Australia
Md Sadek Ferdous	Imperial College London, UK
Mohammad Jabed M. Chowdhury	La Trobe University, Australia
Naipeng Dong	University of Queensland, Australia
Nathan Churchward	Cuscal Limited, Australia

Peter McBurney	King's College London, UK
Peter Robinson	Immutable, Australia
Qiang Tang	University of Sydney, Australia
Raghavendra Ramesh	SupraOracles, Australia
Ranju Mandal	Torrens University, Australia
R. K. Shyamasundar	IIT-Bombay, India
Salil Kanhere	University of New South Wales, Australia
Samantha Tharani Jeyakumar	Griffith University, Australia
Sandra Johnson	ConsenSys, Australia
Shantanu Pal	Deakin University, Australia
Shiping Chen	Data61-CSIRO, Australia
Sushmita Ruj	University of New South Wales, Australia
Thanh-Hai Tran	ConsenSys, Australia
Vincent Gramoli	University of Sydney, Australia
Vishwas Patil	IIT-Bombay, India
Warwick Powell	Queensland University of Technology, Australia
Yinxing Xue	University of Science and Technology of China, China
Zhe Hou	Griffith University, Australia

Additional Reviewers

Jie Dong
Omar Jarkas
Rudrapatna Shyamasundar
Dora Zelenyanszki

Contents

One-Phase Batch Update on Sparse Merkle Trees for Rollups

Boqian Ma⬛, Vir Nath Pathak⬛, Lanping Liu, and Sushmita Ruj$^{(\boxtimes)}$⬛

School of Computer Science and Engineering, University of New South Wales,
Kensington, NSW 2052, Australia
{boqian.ma,vir.pathak,sushmita.ruj}@unsw.edu.au,
lanping.liu@unswalumni.com

Abstract. A sparse Merkle tree is a Merkle tree with fixed height and
indexed leaves given by a map from indices to leaf values. It allows
for both efficient membership and non-membership proofs. It has been
widely used as an authenticated data structure in various applications,
such as layer-2 rollups for blockchains. zkSync Lite, a popular Ethereum
layer-2 rollup solution, uses a sparse Merkle tree to represent the state of
the layer-2 blockchain. The account information is recorded in the leaves
of the tree. In this paper, we study the sparse Merkle tree algorithms presented in zkSync Lite, and propose an efficient batch update algorithm
to calculate a new root hash given a list of account (leaf) operations.
Using the construction in zkSync Lite as a benchmark, our algorithm 1)
improves the account update time from $\mathcal{O}(\log n)$ to $\mathcal{O}(1)$ and 2) reduces
the batch update cost by half using a one-pass traversal. Empirical analysis of real-world block data shows that our algorithm outperforms the
benchmark by at most 14%.

Keywords: Blockchain Scalability · Sparse Merkle Trees · Rollups ·
Layer-2

1 Introduction

Recent advances in distributed ledger technology have introduced a new
paradigm of applications called "decentralisation applications" (DApps) with
new use cases in areas such as finance [7,20], logistics [29], and Internet-of-
Things [26]. However, the increasing number of users and transactions on DApps
has also exposed the key limitation of the scalability of their underlying public
blockchain infrastructures [17]. Two of the largest public blockchians by market
capitalisation[1], Bitcoin [24] and Ethereum [32], can only process 7 and 29 transactions per second (TPS), which is far from their centralised payment provider
counterpart, Visa, which claims to have the capacity to process 65,000 TPS [30].

There are many ways to improve blockchain scalability. They can be broadly
grouped into two categories: on-chain and off-chain. On-chain research involves

---

[1] https://coinmarketcap.com/ accessed on 23rd of August 2023.

N. Dong et al. (Eds.): SDLT 2023, CCIS 1975, pp. 1–21, 2024.
https://doi.org/10.1007/978-981-97-0006-6_1

changing the underlying blockchain infrastructure to achieve better scalability. Examples of on-chain research efforts include developing efficient consensus algorithms [18,28], sharding [23,33], and changing block configurations [13]. On the other hand, off-chain research efforts involve changing how we interact with the blockchain (L1). Instead of performing all activities on-chain, we offload the computation- and storage-intensive activities off-chain. Some existing solutions include State Channels [25], Plasma [27], and rollups [11]. These scaling solutions are known as "Layer-2" (L2) solutions.

The recent developments of L2 rollups such as zkSync Lite [21], Aztec Network [9], Loopering [22], and Immutable X [1] has shown prominent results toward increasing transaction throughput on Ethereum. Rollups execute transactions off-chain and bundle the results of many L2 transactions into one L1 transaction. L1 cannot interpret L2 data, it only acts as a *data availability layer* for L2 activity. Such techniques provide a reduction in computation to L1, while also massively decreasing the transaction fees as one L1 transaction fee is shared amongst all transactions bundled within it.

zkSync Lite [21], a widely used and well-documented zero-knowledge rollup technique, has achieved a maximum observed TPS of 110 [2], making it almost 6 times faster than Ethereum. Following the success of rollups, Ethereum has introduced a rollup-centric roadmap [12] specifically directing future scaling efforts on Ethereum to maximise the use of L2 rollups.

In an L2 rollup, there are generally *operators* keeping the L2 state, processing L2 transactions and communicating with L1 through a smart contract. *Users* have *accounts* and *balances* of tokens. L2 users submit signed transactions to the operators, who then collect those transactions and form L2 blocks.

Sparse Merkle trees (SMT) are widely used as authenticated data structures to keep state information in rollups because of their simplicity and effectiveness. The leaves of SMTs represent account-related information, such as balances and nonce. The root hash of SMTs is a succinct representation of the state of all account balances. Given a block of L2 transactions, the operators will calculate a new root hash based on the result of these transactions. Generally, the process of finding the root hash involves two parts: first, the account leaves need to be updated. Then, the new root hash is calculated by updating the paths from the updated leaves to the root.

The current implementation of this in zkSync Lite is to first go through the transactions in a block sequentially to update the leaves individually and then calculate the root hash. This solution involves traversing the SMTs twice for every updated leaf, which is inefficient. We denote this as a two-phase algorithm.

To build on the above solution, this paper introduces the notion of BatchUpdate on SMTs. The action of *batching* is defined as processing transactions in a block all at once instead of individually. All accounts involved in transactions in a block are updated together in a batch. Instead of traversing the SMTs twice, we propose a new algorithm to update the leaves and intermediate hashes at the same time by traversing the SMTs only once. We name this approach the one-phase batch update (OBU).

Our Contributions

1. We introduce an efficient SMT leaf update algorithm, `SMT.UpdateLeaf`, that improves account update time from $\mathcal{O}(\log n)$ to $\mathcal{O}(1)$.
2. Building on this, an SMT batch update algorithm, `SMT.BatchUpate`, is proposed to calculate the root hash of an SMT, reducing the total number of traversals by 50% from $\mathcal{O}(k \log n) + \mathcal{O}(k \log n)H$ to $\mathcal{O}(k \log n)H$, where k is the number of updates in a batch, n is the total number of leaves in the SMT, and H is a hash operation.[2]
3. Performance analysis of our proposed algorithm was conducted using both micro- and macro-benchmarks in single and multi-threaded scenarios.
4. In real-world macro-benchmark data, our algorithm outperformed the benchmark by up to 14%.

Organisation. The rest of the paper is organised as follows. Section 2 introduces the preliminary information. Next, Sect. 3 discusses some related work. In Sect. 4, we introduce the batch update algorithm. Section 6 outlines our experimental results, followed by the conclusion and discussion in Sect. 7.

2 Preliminaries

2.1 Leaf Operation

Definition 1 (Leaf Operation). *Given a Merkle tree (MT), T, with n leaf nodes $L = \{\text{leaf}_0, \cdots, \text{leaf}_{n-1}\}$ and their corresponding data items $D = \{d_0, \cdots, d_{n-1}\}$ where $\text{leaf}_j = H(d_j)$, a leaf operation $o^j \in \{InsertLeaf, UpdateLeaf, RemoveLeaf\}$ where $0 \leq j < |D|$, is a function that modifies the value of leaf_j. InsertLeaf inserts a new leaf, given by $\text{leaf}_j = H(d_j)$, into the tree, UpdateLeaf updates the value of leaf_j, and RemoveLeaf removes leaf_j and d_j from the tree and D respectively.*

2.2 Sparse Merkle Tree

Definition 2 (Sparse Merkle Tree). *An SMT is an MT with a fixed depth of N, and indexed leaves. Data items $D = \{d_0, \cdots, d_{n-1}\}$ where $n < 2^N$ are stored in a map, $M : \{0,1\}^{2^N} \to D$ mapping from leaf indices to data items. An SMT is defined by the following set of algorithms on M:*

1. *$Gen(N) \to SMT$: Algorithm that generates an empty SMT given a depth N.*
2. *$SMT.Commit(M) \to R'$. Deterministic algorithm that inserts every key-value pair in M into the tree and returns the new root hash.*
3. *$SMT.ApplyOp(o^i) \to R'$ Deterministic algorithm that applies the leaf operation o^i and returns a new root hash R'. $SMT.ApplyOp(o^i)$ can be further categorised into three methods depending on the operation type. They are $SMT.InsertLeaf(o^i)$, $SMT.UpdateLeaf(o^i)$, and $SMT.RemoveLeaf(o^i)$. A description of each of these operations can be found in Sect. 2.1.*

---

[2] Code at: https://github.com/Boqian-Ma/one-phase-batch-update-SMT.

4. *SMT.MemberWitnessCreate(i)* → w_i: *Deterministic algorithm that returns the Merkle proof of $M(i)$ consisting of a list of siblings nodes from* leaf$_i$ *to the root.*
5. *SMT.MemberVerify(w_i, d_i)* → {*true, false*}: *Deterministic algorithm that verifies whether d_i is a member of M.*

SMTs have the same membership-proof construction as regular Merkle trees. However, proving non-membership is more efficient on SMTs than on Merkle trees, since a non-membership for a key k in an SMT is the membership proof of the default value.

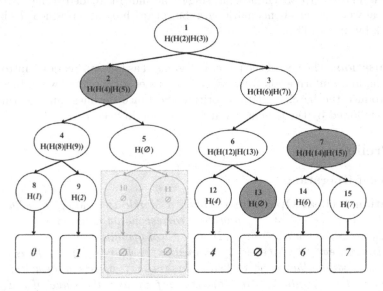

Fig. 1. A SMT of 3 levels. The ovals represent internal nodes. The squares represents its value mapping M, where the numbers are the keys of M and the leaf indices. The default value is represented as ∅. The highlighted nodes form leaf$_4$'s membership proof. Since leaf$_2$ and leaf$_3$ are empty, everything below their highest common parent, node$_5$, are pruned to increase storage efficiency.

Space Optimisation. Instead of storing the full SMT of $2^{N+1} - 1$ nodes, Bauer [10] presents a memory efficient way of storing an SMT by pruning empty sub-trees. Referring to node 5, Fig. 1, following Bauer's proposal, the subtree of node 5 is replaced with the default hash. As such, the space can be greatly reduced.

3   Related Work

This section introduces zkSync Lite [21] and its relevant SMT root hash update algorithm, which we use as our benchmark.

ZkSync Lite. zkSync Lite [21] is an L2 rollup solution developed by Matter Labs [3]. It supports simple transaction types including transfer or swap of ERC-20 [31] tokens, and ERC-721 [15] token minting. Like most L2 solutions, zkSync Lite has two main components: on-chain and off-chain. The on-chain component includes several Solidity Smart Contracts deployed[3] on Ethereum L1. The off-chain component includes several micro-services that facilitate L2 transaction executions and SNARK [16] generation. Detailed descriptions of the zkSync Lite design are given in the Appendix A.1

Account Tree Construction. SMTs are used in three places in zkSync Lite: account tree[4], circuit account tree, and balance tree. The account tree is the main data structure that keeps track of the account balances of its users. The circuit account tree and the balance tree are derived from the account tree and are used to build zero-knowledge block proofs. Here, we give descriptions of the account tree in zkSync Lite.

The account tree is an SMT of depth $N = 24$. As such, it can store up to $2^{25} - 1$ accounts. The accounts are stored in a map M, mapping from leaf indices to accounts. Each internal node, $node_j$, where $1 \leq j \leq 2^{N+1}$, $node_j$'s direct children are $node_j$'s children are given by $node_{2j}$ and $node_{2j+1}$ and $node_j = H(node_{2j} \| node_{2j+1})$. $node_j$ is also known as $node_{2j}$ and $node_{2j+1}$'s parent node. The root of the tree is $node_1$, which also corresponds to the digest of T.

Each leaf node $leaf_k$ where $0 \leq k < 2^N$, corresponds to a key k and is labelled with the value associated with that key if it exists or the hash of a default value otherwise. Formally, if $v = M(k)$ exists, $leaf_k = v$, else $leaf_k = default$, where *default* is a predefined default value.

On the Nth level of SMT (i.e. the leaf level), given by the set of 2^N nodes $\{node_q\}^{2^N}$ where $2^N \leq q < 2^{N+1}$, each $node_j$ corresponds to a key $k = (1 << N) + q$ and is labelled with the hash of the value associated with that key if it exists, or the hash of a default value otherwise. Formally, if $v = M(k)$ exists, $node_q = H(v)$, otherwise $node_q = H(default)$.

For simplicity, we denote the nodes at the leaf level by $L = \{leaf_0, \cdots, leaf_k\}$ where $0 \leq k < 2^N$.

Root Hash Update Algorithm. Here we outline the root hash update algorithm implemented in zkSync Lite given a list of leaf operations. This algorithm is divided into two phases. Consider an account tree T and a list of k operations $O = \{o^j\}_{j \in [0, 2^N)}^k$. The first phase updates the leaves to their new values. For each operation $o^j \in O$, the algorithm traverses T from the root to $leaf_j$ and performs the operation. For example, if o^j was an **update** balance operation, then the balance of $leaf_j$ is updated accordingly. At the end of this phase, all accounts affected by O are updated. Note that when a leaf is updated to a new

---

[3] https://etherscan.io/address/0xaBEA9132b05A70803a4E85094fD0e1800777fBEF.
[4] https://github.com/matter-labs/zksync/blob/master/core/lib/types/src/lib.rs#L84.

value, all nodes in its parent path need to be recomputed. This phase does not concern the hash calculation and takes $\mathcal{O}(k \log n)$ running time to perform k updates.

The second phase re-computes the hashes of affected paths and returns the new root hash. To compute the root hash, the algorithm traverses left and right recursively from T's root to retrieve or compute the child hashes. Recursion terminates when 1) an updated leaf is reached or 2) when all the child leaves of the current nodes are unchanged from the first phase. In case 1), the leaf hash is calculated and returned. In case 2), the current node hash is returned. As a result of this recursive algorithm, the new root hash is calculated. This phase takes $\mathcal{O}(k \log n)H$ running time, where H is the running time of the chosen hash function. Together, the root hash calculation process takes $\mathcal{O}(k \log n) + \mathcal{O}(k \log n)H$.

The first phase occurs in the block producer module, while the second phase occurs in the root hash calculator module. In the actual implementation, these two phases are completed in two separate micro-services. The first phase occurs in the "block producer" module, where the leaves are updates. Then, the second phase happens in the "root hash calculator" module, where the new root hash is computed. This separation takes the hash calculation computation overhead away from the main service.

Inefficiencies. Above we described a two-phase algorithm implemented in zkSync Lite to update the root state of the account tree given a list of k leaf operations. As stated in the zkSync Lite code base[5], there exists a bottleneck that constrains the speed of the block producer producing blocks. If the block producer's speed exceeds the speed of root hash calculation, then the job queue for the root hash calculator will increase indefinitely. Furthermore, we observe that for each operation $o^j \in O$, the path between the updated $leaf_j$ and root is traversed twice. The first traversal occurs when updating the account values and the second time occurs when calculating the root hash.

4   One-Phase Batch Update on Sparse Merkle Tree

In this section, we first outline the basic functionalities of the three leaf operations, SMT.InsertLeaf, SMT.UpdateLeaf and SMT.RemoveLeaf. Then, we introduce a more efficient algorithm, SMT.BatchUpdate(O) $\to R'$ that takes in a list of operations and returns the new SMT root. The pseudocode is outlined in Algorithm 1.

4.1   Leaf Operation Algorithms

1. SMT.InsertLeaf($leaf_j$) is a deterministic algorithm that inserts $leaf_j$ into the SMT by traversing from the root. It has a runtime of $\mathcal{O}(\log n)$.

---

[5] https://github.com/matter-labs/zksync/blob/master/core/bin/zksync_core/src/ state_keeper/root_hash_calculator/mod.rs#L21

2. $SMT.UpdateLeaf(leaf'_j)$ is a deterministic algorithm that updates the value of $leaf_j$ to $leaf'_j$. This algorithm assumes the existence of $v = M(j)$. As such, we can complete this algorithm in $\mathcal{O}(1)$.
3. $SMT.RemoveLeaf(j)$ is a deterministic algorithm that updates the value of $leaf_j$ to *default*. Similar to $SMT.UpdateLeaf$, it assumes the existence of $v = M(j)$ and can be completed in $\mathcal{O}(1)$.

4.2 Batch Update Algorithm

$SMT.BatchUpdate$ is based on bottom-up binary tree level-order traversal using a queue data structure. It is broken down into two parts. In the first part (lines 4–9), we update the leaf nodes. In the second part (lines 10–19), we re-calculate the hashes of nodes in the affected paths in a bottom-up fashion and eventually return the new root hash. **T.cache** is a list of nodes that make up the tree.

Referring to lines 4 to 9, we first initialise an empty set *parent_set*, which we will use to store the indices of the direct parent nodes of the leaves that we updated. We use a set data structure to avoid duplicated parents (i.e. if we update both $node_4$ and $node_5$, then the parent node of both nodes, $node_2$, will only be added to the parent set once). Next, for each $o^j \in O$, we apply o^j to the value $M(j)$, calculate the new hash of $leaf_j = H(M(j))$ and add $leaf_j$'s parent node's index to *parent_set*. As a result of performing all operations, *parent_set* is filled with a set of node indices at a level above the leaf level (i.e. $N - 1$).

Referring to lines 10–19, given parent_set, we first empty them into a queue current_level, which represents the indexes of the nodes we are updating. Next, for each $i \in$ current_level we calculate and update $H(node_i)$ by retrieving i's children hashes $H(node_{2i})$ and $H(node_{2i+1})$ from T. We are guaranteed to retrieve the most recently updated children's hashes because when we process indexes at level n where $0 \leq n \leq N$, nodes in $n + 1$ have already been updated. Then, we add $node_i$'s parent index $node_{\lfloor i/2 \rfloor}$ to *parent_set*. We repeat this process until we reach the root level of T. As a result, $node_1$ (i.e. the root) will be updated and returned.

Example. To illustrate the above algorithm, consider an SMT of depth 2 and a list of operations $O = \{o^0, o^3, o^1\}$. Figure 2 (A) shows the leaf level nodes that are affected by O, they are $L_2 = \{node_4, node_5, node_7\}$ and their corresponding values in M (i.e. $M(0), M(1), M(3)$).

As a result of updating M and re-hashing L_2 nodes, 2.B shows the updated leaf nodes and M, and the parent nodes of L_2 which are $L_1 = \{node_2, node_3\}$ as dotted borders. Now, to re-hash $node_2$, we retrieve $node_2$'s children nodes which are $node'_4$ and $node'_5$. The same can be done for $node_3$. Figure 2 (C) shows the result of re-hashing L_1, and the parent nodes of L_1, which is $node_1$. In the end, Fig. 2 (D) shows the final result of the algorithm and a new root hash.

Algorithm 1. Sparse Merkle Tree Batch Update

1: **Input:** Sparse Merkle Tree **T** of depth N, List of leaf operations $\mathbf{O} = \{o^j\}_{j \in [0,2^N)}^k$ of size k.
2: **Output:** Root Hash **H**
3: **procedure** SMTBATCHUPDATE(**T**, **O**)
4:     parent_set ← Set()
5:     **for all** $o^j \in \mathbf{O}$ **do**
6:         perform operation o^j on leaf$_j$
7:         calculate the new hash of leaf$_j$ and update the value in **T**
8:         parent_set.add(leaf$_j$.parent)
9:     **end for**
10:     **while** parent_set is non-empty **do**
11:         current_level = empty(parent_set)
12:         **for** parent p_i in current_level **do**
13:             left_child_hash = get_child_hash(p_i.left)
14:             right_child_hash = get_child_hash(p_i.right)
15:             calculate the new hash of p_i by using left_child_hash and right_child_hash p_i and update the value in T.
16:             parent_set.add(p_i.parent)
17:         **end for**
18:     **end while**
        return T.cache[ROOT_index]
19: **end procedure**

4.3   Comparison

Table 1 compares the performance of the baseline and OBU for different types of leaf operations, SMT.Commit, and SMT.BatchUpdate. The table assumes an SMT of n leaves and a list of k operations. Although our SMT.BatchUpdate has the same asymptotic time complexity, it is more efficient because the improvement in SMT.UpdateLeaf and SMT.RemoveLeaf. Furthermore, the space complexity of our algorithm remained the same as the baseline algorithm, which is $\mathcal{O}(2^N)$.

Table 1. Asymptotic complexity comparison between OBU and the baseline. n is the number of leaves, k is the number of operations in a block, and H is a hash operation.

Method	zkSync Lite [21]	OBU
SMT.InsertLeaf	$\mathcal{O}(\log n)$	$\mathcal{O}(\log n)$
SMT.UpdateLeaf	$\mathcal{O}(\log n)$	$\boldsymbol{\mathcal{O}(1)}$
SMT.RemoveLeaf	$\mathcal{O}(\log n)$	$\boldsymbol{\mathcal{O}(1)}$
$|w_i|$	$\mathcal{O}(\log n)$	$\mathcal{O}(\log n)$
SMT.Commit	$\mathcal{O}(k \log n)H$	$\mathcal{O}(k \log n)H$
SMT.BatchUpdate	$\mathcal{O}(k \log n) + \mathcal{O}(k \log n)H$	$\mathcal{O}(k \log n)H$

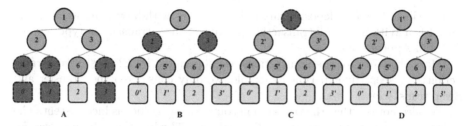

Fig. 2. An illustration of the one-phase batch update example provided in Sect. 4.2. Circle nodes are internal nodes, square nodes are data items with leaf indices, dotted boarders represent the nodes that are currently in the queue, and an apostrophe on a number represents the updated state of a node.

5   Experimental Analysis

We performed both micro- and macro-benchmarks to compare our algorithm with the benchmark. The micro-benchmarks consisted of simple leaf operations in single-threaded and multi-threaded settings. The macro-benchmark compared the performance of the algorithms on real-world block data from zkSync Lite. This section describes the experimental setup, the dataset used for the macro-benchmark, and the multi-threading optimisation for SMT.BatchUpdate.

5.1   Experimental Setup

zkSync Lite is implemented in the Rust programming language [19] as an open source project on Github[6]. We implemented Algorithm 1 on top of the existing repository. Further, we also optimised our implementation for multi-threading computation using the Rayon [4] library in rust.

The experiments are performed on an *AWS c5.12xlarge Debian, 48 CPU, 96 GiB memory* virtual machine. The SMT we used for our experiments has a depth of 24, which is the same depth as the one in zkSync Lite. For each experiment, we performed 10 runs and reported the average run time. The main metric we use to compare performance is the percentage decrease in run time given by

$$\%\text{decrease in running-time} = \frac{\text{new running-time} - \text{old running-time}}{\text{old running-time}}.$$

5.2   Dataset Collection

The macro-benchmark dataset contains 100 (block #299246- #299346) recent blocks and their transactions which are collected through the zkSync Lite API [5] and the zkSync Lite block explorer [6].

Of the 8376 transactions collected, 3971 are swap transactions, 1897 are transfer transactions, 1428 are MintNFT transactions, 766 are ChangePubKey

---

[6]   https://github.com/matter-labs/zksync.

transactions, 266 are deposit transactions, 47 are withdraw transactions, and only 1 is a WithdrawNFT transaction. Details of these transaction types can be found in Appendix C.

More than 70% of the transactions are dominated by ERC-20 token transactions. To keep the experiments simple, we only considered the Transfer and Swap transaction.

We also noticed that the transaction count for each block is inconsistent. The maximum number of transactions observed was 133 while the minimum was 74. This is the result of a combination of the gas limit reached and the appearance of *Priority Transactions* such as Deposit and Withdraw during transaction processing, which will cause the current block to be sealed and committed as soon as it is processed (see Table 2).

We observed that there are many highly active accounts. In block # 299273, out of 92 transactions, one leaf was included in 48 transactions, taking up more than half of the block space. On average, each account produced 2.5 transactions in our dataset (Fig. 3).

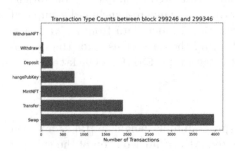

Fig. 3. Transaction count by type between blocks 299264 and 299364

Table 2. Macro-benchmark dataset information of zkSync Lite blocks 299246 - 299346

Statistic	Value
Total # txs	8376
Max tx count in a block	133
min tx count in a block	74
Average tx count in a block	83
Unique accounts	3322
Average tx per account	2.5

5.3 Multi-threading Optimisation

Both the baseline and OBU can be optimised for multi-threading. In the baseline, threads can be created in the recursive stage by visiting the child nodes. In OBU, a thread can be created for every node that requires re-hashing in a level. Note that in the baseline, the threads are nested as the tree is traversed deeper, whereas in OBU, there are no nested threads.

6 Evaluation

6.1 Micro-benchmarks

In Sect. 2.1 we gave three categories of leaf operations: `SMT.UpdateLeaf`, `SMT.InsertLeaf`, and `SMT.RemoveLeaf`. In the micro-benchmarks, we performed simple leaf operations to demonstrate the effectiveness of our pro-

posed algorithm. Without losing generality, we did not include experiments for
SMT.RemoveLeaf operation as the implementation is similar to SMT.UpdateLeaf.

With Multi-threading. Figure 4 shows the performance comparison when
multi-threading is enabled. In Fig. 4 (A1), when the update operations are
applied to leaves with sequential IDs, we see that OBU outperforms the baseline.
We also note that the gap in runtime is increasing by an increasing factor. This
is expected because given k update operations, the baseline spends $\mathcal{O}(k \log n)$
on traversal and update, while with OBU, the update time is linear with respect
to k (i.e. $\mathcal{O}(k)$ update time).

In Fig. 4 (A2), we see that when the number of operations is small, we see
a larger percentage decrease in running time and as the number of operations
increases (10% decreases for 1000 updates), % decrease in running time shows
exponential decay. The initial large percentage decrease relates to how the two
algorithms use multi-threading. In the baseline, threads can be nested as deep as
24 levels, which can cause high computation overhead, whereas in OBU, there
is no such problem because threads end when the currently traversed level is
finished. Furthermore, the diminishing trend in Fig. 4 (A2) can be explained by
hardware limitations. In OBU, as the number of nodes we process on each level
increases, the number of concurrent threads becomes insignificant compared to
the number of nodes we need to process.

Figure 4 (B1) shows the runtime difference when the update operations are
applied to random leaf IDs taken from a uniform distribution. We note that
the improvement in runtime is worse visually compared to Fig. 4 (A1). This is
because when leaf IDs are randomly assigned, there are fewer common parents.
As such, the amount of computation of OBU approaches the baseline. However,
we also note that the trend shown in Fig. 4 (B2) is consistent with Fig. 4 (A2)
when it comes to the percentage of decrease in running time.

Figure 4 (C1) shows the runtime difference for when insert operations are
applied to leaves with sequential IDs. Both Fig. 4 (C1) and Fig. 4 (C2) show
consistent trends as Fig. 4 (A1) and Fig. 4 (A2) respectively.

Without Multi-threading. Figure 5 (A) shows the running time comparison
between the benchmark and OBU when running on a single thread. We note
that there is no visible performance improvement because the tree traversal
time $\mathcal{O}(k \log n)$ is insignificant compared to the hashing time. This is further
demonstrated in Fig. 5 (B) when we only observe a slight improvement in the
percentage decrease in running time.

6.2   Macro-benchmark

We macro-benchmark the performance of OBU with the baseline using zkSync
Lite block data. As shown in Fig. 6, OBU almost always outperforms the baseline.
Overall, OBU performed, on average, 5.12% faster than the baseline, with the

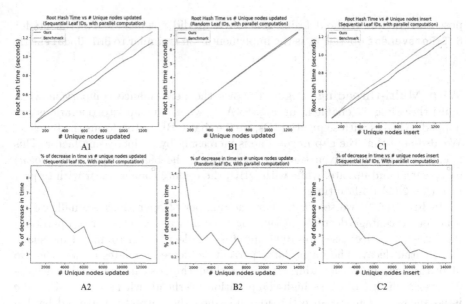

Fig. 4. Top row: root hash time in seconds comparison between benchmark and OBU with various operation types. Bottom row: percentage decrease in root hash time with various operation types. (with multi-threading)

highest percentage of decrease in time being 14%. Next, we analysed the blocks that exhibited the highest/lowest performance improvement. Our observations are as follows:

1. In the block with large percentage of decrease in time (i.e. in solid circles in Fig. 6) we notice that most transactions in the block affected very few accounts. This corresponds to a faster running time because OBU does not repeatedly traverse the same account
2. In the blocks with negative percentage of decrease in time (i.e. in dotted circles in Fig. 6), updates are spread across multiple accounts instead of just a few accounts.

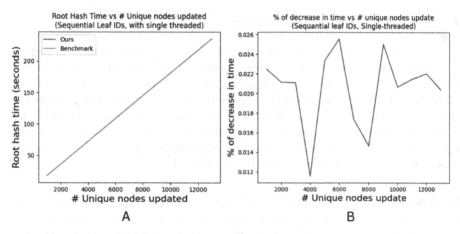

Fig. 5. A) Update operations on leaves with sequential leaf IDs performance comparison, no visible difference. B) Percentage decrease in running time with OBU compared with baseline. (Single-threaded)

Table 3. Result statistics from the macro-benchmark.

Statistic	Runtime Reduction (%, ms)
Mean	5.12%, 25.56
Medium	5.24%, 26.73
Standard Deviation	4.39%, 21.55
Variance	19.24%, 464.68
Minimum	-3.81%, -20.67
Maximum	14.99%, 69.79
Range	18.80%, 90.46

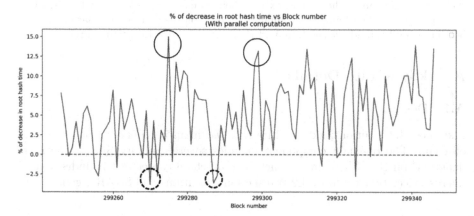

Fig. 6. Percentage decrease in running time on zkSync Lite block data. The dotted horizontal line is when the percentage of decrease is 0.

7 Conclusion and Discussion

In this paper, we presented and evaluated OBU, a batch update algorithm on sparse Merkle trees. The improvement can be summarised as follows. OBU achieved a 50% decrease in run time by traversing the tree once instead of twice. OBU uses threads more efficiently compared to the implementation presented in zkSync Lite. This could reduce the hardware requirement to run an L2 operator. More specifically, OBU reduced the run time by 50% for the SMT.InsertLeaf operation. For SMT.UpdateLeaf and SMT.RemoveLeaf operations, the running time is reduced from $\mathcal{O}(\log n)$ to $\mathcal{O}(1)$ (see Table 1).

High Frequency Transaction Applications. The second improvement will directly benefit applications with a higher frequency of transactions. Suppose that a block has k transactions that affect a single account. Instead of traversing the SMT k times in $\mathcal{O}(k \log n)$ runtime, OBU will complete the operations in $\mathcal{O}(k)$ runtime. This is evident in block #299275[7] where 29 of the 47 transfer/swap transactions in block. In this case, OBU achieved a 14.9% decrease in running time.

7.1 Future Work

For future work, we first want to perform more integration tests in zkSync Lite to better understand the advantages and drawbacks of OBU. Next, we wish to see how our research can improve zkEVM, which is another prominent blockchain scaling direction. Then, we want to see how our research may be used for batch update in other authenticated data structures, such as Vector Commitment schemes [14].

Acknowledgement. The authors extend their thanks to Sean Morota Chu, Ziyu Liu, Nhi Nguyen, and Tim Yang for invaluable feedback on the manuscript, Barak Saini for helping us understand zkSync Lite, and Hao Ren for LaTeX formatting advice.

A zkSync Lite Details

A.1 Design

Like most L2 solutions, zkSync Lite has two main components: on-chain and off-chain. The on-chain component includes several Solidity Smart Contracts deployed[8] on the Ethereum mainnet. The off-chain component includes several microservices that facilitate L2 transaction executions and SNARK generation.

---

[7] https://zkscan.io/explorer/blocks/299275.
[8] https://etherscan.io/address/0xaBEA9132b05A70803a4E85094fD0e1800777fBEF.

A.2   On-Chain

The on-chain component has three main contracts.

The first one is the zkSync main contract. It stores L1 user funds, bridges funds between L1 and L2 with Deposit and Withdraw transactions, accepts committed blocks and block proofs from the operator, verifies block proofs, and process withdrawal transactions by executing blocks. Users can deposit \$ETH or ERC-20 tokens. However, the allowed ERC-20 tokens are determined by the Security Council.

The second Smart Contract is Verifier. Given a committed block and a proof, the Verifier contract verifies the proof to determine the validity of the state transition caused by the transactions in the block.

The third Smart Contract is Governance. It has the functionalities to add (but not remove) ERC-20 tokens to the whitelisted tokens, change the set of operators, and initiate the upgrade of the contracts.

When L1 users wish to deposit/withdraw their funds to/from L2, they can interact directly with the zkSync main contract.

A.3   Off-Chain

The off-chain component is divided into two main sub-components. The server and the prover. An operator needs to run both sub-components in order to create L2 blocks.

Server. The Server has the following modules [21]:

1. Ethereum Watcher: module to monitor on-chain operations.
2. State Keeper: module to execute and seal blocks.
3. Memory Pool: module to organise incoming transactions.
4. Block Proposer: module to create block proposals for state keeper
5. Committer: module to store pending and completed blocks into the database
6. API: module to allow users to interect with zkSync Lite to query block data or submit transactions.
7. Ethereum Sender: module to sync the operations on zkSync Lite with the Ethereum blockchain. It makes sure that the L1 transactions zkSync Lite created (such as committing a block on-chain) are executed on-chain in the correct order.

Prover. The Prover's only job is to create block proofs given a block's transaction witnesses. It regularly polls the Server for blocks that do not have a corresponding SNARK. When a new block is available, Server sends the block's witnesses so the Prover can begin creating the block proof. Once finished, the Prover returns the SNARK to the Server and the server sends it to the on-chain Smart Contract to be verified.

B   zkSync Lite Transaction Flow

Below we describe the transaction flow on zkSync. First, we provide an end-to-end description from L2 transaction submission to L2 block finalisation on-chain. Then, we zoom in on the Server to describe the flow within the Server in details.

B.1   Overall Transaction Flow

Referring to Fig. 7 for a simplified representation of zkSync Lite. When a user submits a transaction, it is placed into the memory pool (mempool) waiting to be collected by the Server. The server periodically collects a queue of transactions from the mempool, in submission order, and puts them into blocks. After the blocks are formed, they are committed to the L1 Smart Contract and stored in the database. At this moment, although the block information is on-chain, they are not finalised. These blocks in this state are known as the "committed block".

At the same time, available Provers poll the Operator for proof generation jobs. When there are blocks without a proof, the Operator will generate and send the block witnesses to the Prover, who will use the witnesses to generate and return the block proof. Once the operator receives the block proof, it will send it to the L1 Smart Contract for verification.

The Verifier contract verifies the block proof along with the committed block data. The L2 Smart Contracts updates the block's from committed to finalised when the proof is validated.

For priority transactions (listed in Sect. C) that are submitted directly to the L1 Smart Contract, they are tracked by the Operator and added to the mempool into a priority queue.

B.2   Transaction Flow Within Server

Looking specifically into the Server shown in Fig. 8, as blocks are created by the block producer, they are sent to the State Keeper. The State Keeper processes the transactions in the blocks and update the accounts' balances accordingly. Although it stores the Account Tree, it does not update the Account Tree's root hash. It delegates the computation intensive job to the Root Hash Calculator, where the re-hashing of the tree is done. Once a block is completed with a root hash, it is committed to the database.

As the Prover polls for committed blocks, the Witness Generator will generate transaction witnesses and send to the Prover.

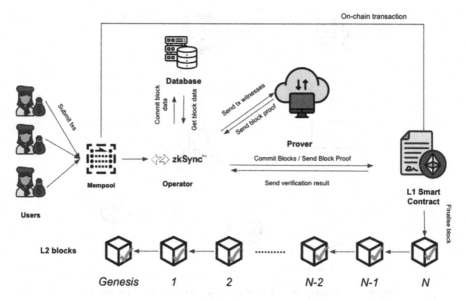

Fig. 7. An illustration of transaction flow within zkSync Lite from transaction submission to L2 block finalisation.

C   zkSync Transaction Types

As mentioned above, zkSync Lite supports a number of transaction types. Here, we give a brief description of these transaction types. Full descriptions can be found in [21]. There are two main categories of transactions on zkSync: normal and priority transactions. Priority transactions are handled by the operator differently during the L2 block creation process. Given a queue of transactions from the mempool, and an operator continually placing transactions into blocks, as soon as a priority transaction is processed, the current block is sealed and committed regardless of remaining gas in the block.

C.1   From Transactions to Leaf Operations

One or more accounts can be affected as a result of a transaction. For example, a transfer transaction adds to the receiver's balance, as well as deducting from the sender's balance. To make the account leaf updates atomic, zkSync breaks down each type of transactions into their a number of *leaf operations*. Each operation only affects one account leaf at a time.

In the following sections, as we describe the transaction types, we include the number of operations to which they can be broken down.

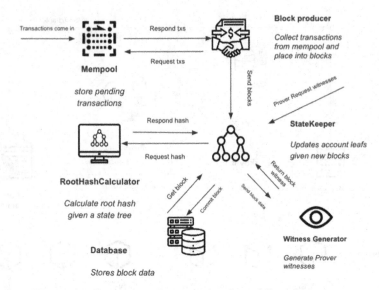

Fig. 8. An illustration of transaction flow zkSync Lite server.

C.2   Normal Transaction Types

1. `Transfer`: Transfer funds between rollup accounts. It translates to two `SMT.UpdateLeaf` operations. The first decreases the sender balance, and the second increases the receiver balance.

2. `Transfer to new`: Transfer funds to a new account. This transaction type is derived from `Transfer` and happens when the to_account doesn't exist in the `AccountTree`. Before the transfer of funds, a new account will be created for to_account. It translates to an *update* and an `SMT.InsertLeaf` operation. The first one decreases sender balance, and the second one inserts a new account leaf.

3. `Withdraw`: Withdraw funds from the L2 account to the indicated Ethereum address. It translates to an `SMT.UpdateLeaf` operation where the balance of the withdrawal account is decreased.

4. `Withdraw NFT`: Withdraw NFT from the L2 account to the indicated Ethereum address. It translates to two `SMT.UpdateLeaf` operations. The first removes the NFT from the owner account and the second removes the NFT from the creator's account.

5. `Mint NFT`: Mint an NFT token inside L2. It translates to two `SMT.UpdateLeaf` operations. The first adds the NFT to the receiver's account, and the second updates the creator's account.

6. `Change pubkey`: Change the public key used to authorise transactions for an account. This can be useful when a user wishes to delegate the account to another user or Smart Contract wallet with a different Ethereum address without the need to expose their own private key. It translates to an `SMT.UpdateLeaf` operation on the sender's account where the public key is updated.

7. `Forced Exit`: Withdraw funds from L2 accounts without the signing key to the appropriate L1 address. These accounts are known as *unowned* accounts. It translates to `SMT.UpdateLeaf` and `SMT.RemoveLeaf` operations. The first up decreases the sender's balance, and the second one removes the account leaf and replaces it with a default node.
8. `Swap`: Perform an atomic swap of ERC-20 tokens between two L2 accounts at a defined ratio. Its operations are similar to the `transfer` transaction type.

C.3   Priority Transaction Types

1. `Deposit`: Deposit funds from Ethereum to L2. The funds are sent to the zkSync Lite Smart Contract, which informs the operator to include a deposit transaction in the next block. A new account is created if necessary. It may translate to an `SMT.UpdateLeaf` operation, or an `SMT.InsertLeaf` operations. The operation is `SMT.UpdateLeaf` when the account already exists. On the other hand, the operation is `SMT.InsertLeaf` when a new account needs to be created.
2. `Full exit`: In the event that a user thinks the operator has censored their transactions, they can submit a `Full exit` transaction directly to the Smart Contract. The operator will process the transaction accordingly. Its operations are the same as `Forced exit`

In the event that a priority transaction has not been processed for more than a week, the system will enter the **exodus mode** and the operators will stop working, and every user can use an exit tool[9] to withdraw their asset by submitting a proof of balance to the L1 smart contract.

D   zkSync Lite Sparse Merkle Tree Usage

zkSync Lite uses the SMT in three separate places as a data accumulator. They are the account tree, the circuit account tree, and the balance tree.

Account Tree. The Account Tree[10] is a binary SMT of depth 24. It is the main data structure that stores the state of the zkSync Lite accounts. Its leaves are the accounts on zkSync. The leaf hash is the rescue hash [8] of an account's fields concatenated in their respective little-endian bit representation.

The leaf indices are the same as the account IDs, which are mapped to account addresses. Empty leaves are replaced with a default hash.

---

[9] https://github.com/matter-labs/zksync/tree/master/infrastructure/exit-tool.
[10] https://github.com/matter-labs/zksync/blob/master/core/lib/types/src/lib.rs# L84.

Circuit Account Tree. The purpose of the Circuit AccountTree is to generate compatible transaction witnesses so that the Prover can create the block proof. The Circuit Account Tree is structured similar to the AccountTree except for two main differences: 1) account data are encoded as field elements and 2) each account uses an SMT to track balances for each type of token (Balance Tree) instead of using a simple hash map. The Circuit AccountTree is derived from AccountTree.

Balance Tree. As mentioned above, the Balance Tree is a part of the account leaves in the Circuit Account Tree. It is an SMT of depth 8. Each leaf in the Balance Tree represents the balance of the token with the id the same as the leaf index.

References

1. https://www.immutable.com/products/immutable-x
2. https://ethtps.info/
3. https://matter-labs.io/
4. https://github.com/rayon-rs/rayon
5. https://docs.zksync.io/api/
6. https://explorer.zksync.io/
7. Adams, H., Zinsmeister, N., Salem, M., Keefer, R., Robinson, D.: Uniswap v3 core. Technical report, Uniswap, Technical Report (2021)
8. Aly, A., Ashur, T., Ben-Sasson, E., Dhooghe, S., Szepieniec, A.: Design of symmetric-key primitives for advanced cryptographic protocols. IACR Trans. Symmetric Cryptol., 1–45 (2020)
9. Aztec: https://aztec.network/
10. Bauer, M.: Proofs of zero knowledge. arXiv preprint: cs/0406058 (2004)
11. Buterin, V.: An incomplete guide to rollups (2020). https://vitalik.ca/general/2021/01/05/rollup.html
12. Buterin, V.: A rollup-centric Ethereum roadmap (2020). https://ethereum-magicians.org/t/a-rollup-centric-ethereum-roadmap/4698/1
13. Buterin, V.: The limits to blockchain scalability (2021). https://vitalik.ca/general/2021/05/23/scaling.html
14. Catalano, D., Fiore, D.: Vector commitments and their applications. In: Kurosawa, K., Hanaoka, G. (eds.) PKC 2013. LNCS, vol. 7778, pp. 55–72. Springer, Heidelberg (2013). https://doi.org/10.1007/978-3-642-36362-7_5
15. Entriken, W., Shirley, D., Sachs, N.: ERC-721: non-fungible token standard. Ethereum Improvement Proposals, no. 721 (2018)
16. Gabizon, A., Williamson, Z.J., Ciobotaru, O.: PLONK: permutations over Lagrange-bases for Oecumenical noninteractive arguments of knowledge. Cryptol. ePrint Arch. (2019)
17. Khan, D., Jung, L.T., Hashmani, M.A.: Systematic literature review of challenges in blockchain scalability. Appl. Sci. **11**(20), 9372 (2021)
18. Kiayias, A., Russell, A., David, B., Oliynykov, R.: Ouroboros: a provably secure proof-of-stake blockchain protocol. In: Katz, J., Shacham, H. (eds.) CRYPTO 2017. LNCS, vol. 10401, pp. 357–388. Springer, Cham (2017). https://doi.org/10.1007/978-3-319-63688-7_12

19. Klabnik, S., Nichols, C.: The Rust Programming Language. No Starch Press, San Francisco (2023)
20. Kumar, M., Nikhil, N., Singh, R.: Decentralising finance using decentralised blockchain oracles. In: 2020 International Conference for Emerging Technology (INCET), pp. 1–4. IEEE (2020)
21. Labs, M.: zkSync: scaling and privacy engine for Ethereum (2020). https://github.com/matter-labs/zksync
22. Loopring: https://loopring.org/
23. Luu, L., Narayanan, V., Zheng, C., Baweja, K., Gilbert, S., Saxena, P.: A secure sharding protocol for open blockchains. In: Proceedings of the 2016 ACM SIGSAC Conference on Computer and Communications Security, pp. 17–30 (2016)
24. Nakamoto, S.: Bitcoin: a peer-to-peer electronic cash system. Decentralized Business Review, p. 21260 (2008)
25. Negka, L.D., Spathoulas, G.P.: Blockchain state channels: a state of the art. IEEE Access 9, 160277–160298 (2021)
26. Panarello, A., Tapas, N., Merlino, G., Longo, F., Puliafito, A.: Blockchain and IoT integration: a systematic survey. Sensors 18(8), 2575 (2018)
27. Poon, J., Buterin, V.: Plasma: scalable autonomous smart contracts. White pap., 1–47 (2017)
28. Rocket, T., Yin, M., Sekniqi, K., van Renesse, R., Sirer, E.G.: Scalable and probabilistic leaderless BFT consensus through metastability. arXiv preprint: arXiv:1906.08936 (2019)
29. Tijan, E., Aksentijević, S., Ivanić, K., Jardas, M.: Blockchain technology implementation in logistics. Sustainability 11(4), 1185 (2019)
30. Visa: https://www.visa.co.uk/dam/VCOM/download/corporate/media/visanet-technology/aboutvisafactsheet.pdf
31. Vogelsteller, F., Buterin, V.: ERC-20: token standard. Ethereum Improvement Proposals, no. 20 (2015)
32. Wood, G., et al.: Ethereum: a secure decentralised generalised transaction ledger
33. Zamani, M., Movahedi, M., Raykova, M.: RapidChain: scaling blockchain via full sharding. In: Proceedings of the 2018 ACM SIGSAC Conference on Computer and Communications Security, pp. 931–948 (2018)

On the Relevance of Blockchain Evaluations on Bare Metal

Andrei Lebedev[1]([✉])[iD] and Vincent Gramoli[1,2]([✉])[iD]

[1] University of Sydney, Sydney, Australia
andrei.lebedev@sydney.edu.au
[2] Redbelly Network, Sydney, Australia
vincent.gramoli@sydney.edu.au

Abstract. In this paper, we present the first bare metal comparison of modern blockchains, including Algorand, Avalanche, Diem, Ethereum, Quorum and Solana. This evaluation was conducted with the recent Diablo benchmark suite [12], a framework to evaluate the performance of different blockchains on the same ground. By tuning network delays in our controlled environment we were able to reproduce performance trends obtained in geo-distributed settings, hence demonstrating the relevance of bare metal evaluations to better understand blockchain performance.

Keywords: Latency · Virtualization · Distributed ledger technologies

1 Introduction

In recent years, there has been a significant increase in the variety of available blockchain protocols, finding applications in various domains such as finance, supply chain management, and healthcare [24]. These diverse use cases give rise to distinct system requirements, encompassing factors like participation types and transaction metrics, particularly when subjected to varying workloads. At the same time, these blockchain protocols are structured with multiple layers, including the membership selection layer, consensus layer, data layer, and execution layer [8,15], each precisely tailored to address specific utilization scenarios.

In the process of selecting appropriate blockchain protocols, system developers are tasked with making well-informed decisions by considering the array of available options, each tailored to specific layers in line with their particular requirements.

To facilitate this decision-making, benchmarking has emerged as a valuable tool to assess various systems [23]. Both protocol developers and researchers contribute to this evaluation process by reporting metrics such as transaction throughput, latency, and resource utilization. However, it is important to note that the evaluation environment itself can vary significantly across different experiments. These variations encompass a range of scenarios, from utilizing Internet of Things (IoT) devices to leveraging high-performance computing clusters [13], which could be situated in a single datacenter or distributed across various remote locations.

N. Dong et al. (Eds.): SDLT 2023, CCIS 1975, pp. 22–38, 2024.
https://doi.org/10.1007/978-981-97-0006-6_2

Researchers evaluated the protocols in various experiments using bare metal clusters [14,18,20], yet an area that remains relatively unexplored is the influence of network equipment on these setups. While the majority of the studies consider average latency [12], blockchain experiments often overlook a notable aspect that is the tail latency [6], which can provide more comprehensive insights into performance. It is worth noting that some authors have taken steps to emulate a geo-distributed environment [17], but a critical gap exists in terms of directly comparing results from these emulations to those obtained within a standard network, using identical workloads. Bridging this gap and conducting a side-by-side assessment of these two distinct environments under the same experimental conditions would yield valuable insights into the performance and viability of blockchain implementations across different network configurations.

In this paper, we present the first bare metal comparison of modern blockchains. To this end, we evaluate six blockchains, Algorand [10], Avalanche [19], Diem [1], Ethereum [25], Quorum [4] and Solana [26] with the recent Diablo [12] benchmark suite in a cluster. We make the following contributions:

- The performance trends obtained on our cluster with artificial network delays are similar to the ones obtained on geo-distributed settings. In the Testnet and Devnet configurations, Solana provides similar performance and this was observed on the cluster as well as in a geo-distributed virtualized environment of previous work. Diem provides higher throughput for Testnet than for Devnet as observed in both the cluster and the geo-distributed virtualized environment.
- We show that switches in the LAN do not impact the performance of blockchain significantly. This is explained by the blockchain latencies being in the order of the second whereas the switches would impact services with latencies orders of magnitude smaller (of the order of the millisecond).
- We show that the average blockchain transaction latency is generally not representative of its tail latency. In particular, Algorand and Quorum would typically have a significantly larger tail latency than average latency under 1000 TPS and 10,000 TPS workloads. While Solana does not experience much difference in our experiments, the difference on Avalanche and Diem can be high as well.

This paper is organised as follows. Section 2 describes the differences in local and cloud environments, and lists the benefits and the drawbacks of each setting. In Sect. 3, we demonstrate the performance of the 6 blockchain protocols in the local testbed, focusing on the impact of network switches, number of blockchain nodes, and the network delay between them. Section 4 looks at the different aspects of the evaluation which can be taken into account in order to increase the depth of understanding of the blockchain protocols. We discuss the related work in Sect. 5 and conclude the paper in Sect. 6.

2 Analysis

In this section, we look into the differences of cloud provided virtual machines
and local testbeds on the example of Amazon Web Services (AWS) and the i8
chair testbed.

2.1 Cloud Environments

The cloud environments provide certain benefits for the blockchain protocol evaluation. One of the important points is scalability in terms of computing power.
Amazon Web Services (AWS) provide a vast range of machine types, for example,
from 2 vCPUs and 4 GB RAM to 96 vCPUs and 192 GB RAM. Protocols can be
optimized for different hardware with multiprocessing capabilities, such as GPU
and CPU with vector extensions or CPU with specific architecture. Such factors
are taken into account by the providers, and machines with different hardware
are also available.

While multiple machines of different types can be spawned in the same datacenter, cloud providers also typically have multiple datacenters across the globe.
This brings us to the second benefit of AWS, which is geographical distribution. Currently, Amazon has AWS datacenters in more than ten regions. With
this feature, we can create networks of hundreds of machines, which allows us
to easily test the scalability aspect of the protocol in terms of the number of
blockchain nodes.

The fact that the datacenters are distributed across the globe provides us with
a network with realistic latency and bandwidth. Even though virtualization is
present in the setup, the machines share the actual hardware and network links.
As the datacenters are located on different continents, we are provided with the
latencies limited by the physical properties of the connection and the actual
distance and underlying network topology between the locations. As different
services on the machines communicate with each other and are accessed by
the users, the bandwidth of the links is being used. This allows taking another
important aspect of real networks into account during the evaluation, which is
background traffic.

However, such an environment makes it hard to perform reproducible tests.
The utilization of the network links between the datacenters changes throughout
the day, as the services may be accessed more during the day and less at night.
The usage is reflected in latency and bandwidth, with lower latency and higher
bandwidth available at hours with reduced usage and higher round-trip time
(RTT) and lower throughput being observed at peak usage hours.

2.2 Local Testbeds

In order to account for the variance in the network parameters, local testbeds can
be used to perform the measurements. In this environment, the whole network
can be exclusively used by the system under test. For example, with the iLab
testbed, we have measured an average of 1.1 ms RTT using the same approach

as with AWS. Given that the latency between the nodes does not change, we can introduce arbitrary delays to evaluate the tolerance of the blockchain protocol against the network delays.

Such property of the iLab testbed network as fixed latency between the nodes allows us to replicate the latencies of geographically distributed cloud networks at a particular point in time. With `tc-netem` tool, we can specify the added delay on a network interface of the machine used for running the experiments. Ideally, such a setup can be used to reduce the usage of cloud environments, produce similar results, and reduce the cost of the experiments.

In order for the deployment solution to be backend-independent, it should operate on a unified protocol, such as SSH. In this case, it will be possible to operate on any set of servers that are accessible with SSH on the host.

3   Evaluation

In this section, we evaluate six blockchain protocols with Diablo on the local testbed environment.

Diablo [12] is a blockchain benchmarking framework that allows comparing different protocols on the same ground with realistic workloads based on real application traces. Diablo has master-worker architecture, where *Primary* acts as an orchestrator and result aggregator, and *Secondaries* produce the workload and collect results for individual transactions. Diablo is accompanied by a set of scripts called Minion [11] that allows to automate the experiments.

The rationale for choosing the blockchain protocols is that they represent various consensus algorithms and virtual machines with different properties. Avalanche and Algorand offer probabilistic consensus algorithms, Diem and Quorum use variants of deterministic Byzantine fault tolerant consensus algorithms, and Ethereum and Solana use eventually consistent consensus algorithms. From the virtual machine perspective, Avalanche, Quorum, and Ethereum use Ethereum Virtual Machine and Solidity programming language, which Solana also makes use of with the Solang compiler. Algorand features Transaction Execution Approval language and Algorand Virtual machine, and Diem provides smart contract capabilities with Move programming language and MoveVM.

To run the experiments on the iLab [16] testbed, we use `eth-static` interface, which is a dedicated 10 gigabit network between all the testbed machines. As shown in Fig. 1, the network consists of 7 groups of machines called isles (named A, B, C, D, E, F, S) of 6 machines each, plus an isle of 3 machines (named R), giving 8 isles and 45 machines in total. Every two isles (A and S, B and R, C and D, E and F) are connected to a switch, and there are overall 4 switches, and all of them are connected to each other. We interface Minion with Plain Orchestration Service [9] to allocate and deploy the machines.

The machines have the following hardware:

- Intel Core i7-8700 CPU @ 3.20 GHz (6/12 cores/threads)
- 64 GB RAM

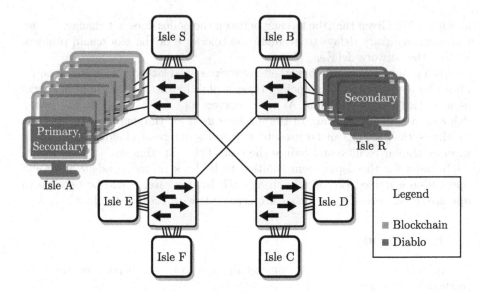

Fig. 1. iLab topology

- 500 GB SSD
- Intel X550T 10 GbE NIC
- Debian 11 Bullseye

To distribute the workload generation over the testbed, we spread the Secondaries across all the available isles. We use the first machines of isles A-S and the machines of isle R for workload generation, giving us 10 machines for Secondaries in total. We use the remaining machines for blockchain nodes in different configurations. For simplicity, we vary the number of blockchain nodes as a multiple of 5, since we have 5 machines left from isles A-S. Same as in AWS setup, for the Primary, we use one of the machines which run the Secondary, as the Primary does not use any resources when the workload is applied to the blockchain network.

3.1   Inter-switch Communication

With the local testbed, we focus on finer-grained small-scale experiments which look into how the network scales when the number of blockchain nodes is increased and how the network delay affects the performance of the protocols.

As we have two isles connected to a single switch, we have multiple possible configurations with the experiments involving two, four, or six isles. With two isles, they can either be connected to a single switch or be connected to two different switches. With four isles, two switches can be fully utilized, or there can be a partial utilization of three or four switches. With six isles, either three or four switches can be used. All of these configurations may affect the performance of the blockchain network.

In the next experiments, we send a constant workload of native transfer transactions over 2 min to the blockchain network.

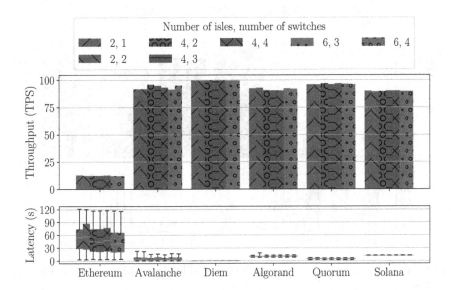

Fig. 2. Throughput and latency, 100 TPS workload, varied number of isles and switches

Figure 2 shows the throughput and latency for each blockchain when stressed with a workload of 100 TPS. We can see that for all of the protocols, the measured throughput stays consistent and is not affected by possible delays added by the switches. For Ethereum, we see a slight decrease in the median latency as we scale up the number of blockchain nodes. We observe that Ethereum achieves significantly lower throughput and displays high latency variance, which can be caused by the default 15 s `block-period` parameter of Ethereum Clique consensus algorithm.

Next, we experiment with the same setups and a workload of 1,000 TPS in Fig. 3. Here we start to notice a significant variance in results compared to the previous experiment. First, Avalanche fails to handle the workload, and the latency for the transactions the network manages to commit jumps from 7 s to 53 s, which is a 7.6 times increase in the average latency. Such behavior could be caused by the default block production configuration, if it is optimized for lower throughput. We also notice that the maximum latency of committed transactions in Quorum starts to depend on the number of nodes. The higher maximum latency means that certain transactions remain in the mempool for longer periods of time, which might be caused by the round-robin block proposer selection.

Lastly, in Fig. 4, we present the results of the experiments with the same setups and a workload of 10,000 TPS. Here, Solana shows the best results with regard to handling a very high workload. While Quorum exhibits low latency,

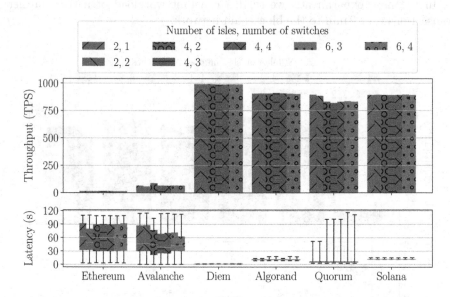

Fig. 3. Throughput and latency, 1,000 TPS workload, varied number of isles and switches

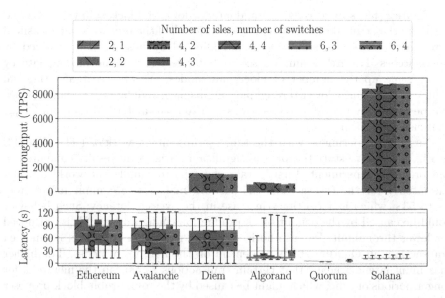

Fig. 4. Throughput and latency, 10,000 TPS workload, varied number of isles and switches

the throughput is significantly lower than the workload, what might be explained by the internal data structures being oversaturated, and client requests being dropped.

Overall, we make a conclusion that the number of switches does not affect our measurements in a noticeable way and proceed to use the configuration with the minimal number of switches in the next experiments.

3.2 Isle Scalability

To evaluate the scalability of the blockchain protocols in terms of the size of the network, we create networks of sizes 5 (1 isle), 10 (2 isles), 20 (4 isles), 30 (6 isles), and 35 (7 isles). We fully utilize the testbed, as it consists of 45 machines in total. We stress the network with the constant workload of native transfer transactions over 2 min with a varied rate.

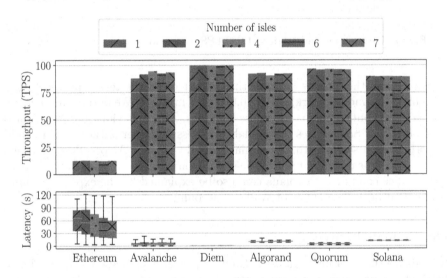

Fig. 5. Throughput and latency, 100 TPS workload, varied number of isles

In Fig. 5, we compare the latency and the throughput of each protocol under the constant workload of 100 TPS. We again note that the measured throughput stays consistent between the different sizes of the network for all the blockchains. With Ethereum, we notice a pattern that the median latency tends to become smaller as the network size increases. We cannot increase the size of the network to observe the behavior further. However, the decrease becomes smaller with each network size increase.

Figure 6 shows the latency and the throughput for the blockchain protocols under test with the 1,000 TPS workload. The maximum observed latency in Quorum tends to increase with the size of the network. However, at the same time, the throughput does not have a noticeable impact.

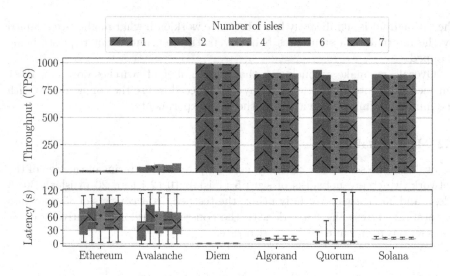

Fig. 6. Throughput and latency, 1,000 TPS workload, varied number of isles

We display the latency and the throughput of all the tested protocols in 7 configurations under a workload of 10,000 TPS in Fig. 7. We observe an increase in the throughput in Solana as we use 20 nodes. This behavior can be explained by the fact that Solana uses the available processing power of the machines, and its performance scales with the available hardware. For Algorand, we reached its announced peak throughput in the experiment. For Diem, the relatively poor performance compared to Solana can also be explained by the experiment limitation regarding the number of available accounts.

3.3   Emulated Latency

To evaluate the tolerance against network delays and simulate a real-world geo-distributed environment, we use a network of 35 machines, 7 isles in total. Each of the isles represents a separate location with a fixed delay to other locations. For simplicity, we use equal delay values for all the isles. We experiment with delays of 50, 100, 150, 200, 250, and 300 milliseconds.

Table 1. Added and average measured RTT (ms) between the isles

Added	0	50	100	150	200	250	300
Measured	1.13814	49.758	99.663	149.689	199.73	249.782	299.727

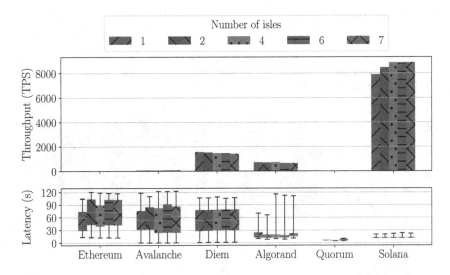

Fig. 7. Throughput and latency, 10,000 TPS workload, varied number of isles

In Table 1, we compare the added and measured RTT between the isles in the testbed to verify that the changes we did with tc are correctly applied in the whole network. We see the measured values slightly below the target value because we subtracted the baseline RTT from the added value as we were making the changes.

In Fig. 8, we compare the throughput and the latency of the protocols under test with 100 TPS workload, and varied added delay between the isles. We can notice that the performance of Algorand and Quorum stays consistent regardless of the added delay. For Solana, the median latency increases from 12.01 to 14.53 milliseconds. The important observation is that the Diem performance drops significantly with the added delay, and the throughput decreases by more than 50%. We can infer from the observation that the protocol was optimized for low-latency setups and is not suitable for real-world networks in the current state.

We display the latency and the throughput for all the tested protocols with 1,000 TPS workload in Fig. 9. Compared to the previous workload, we see that the throughput of Quorum is halved as we add even 50 millisecond delay between the isles. At the same time, the latency stays the same for the different delay settings. For Diem, we see the same behavior of decreased throughput and increased latency. For the other protocols, the performance stays consistent with the increase of the delay in the network.

Figure 10 shows the throughput and the latency measures for the protocols under the 10,000 TPS workload. As before, Ethereum and Avalanche show minimal throughput, and Quorum fails to handle the provided workload. We notice the same performance drop for Diem. Solana and Algorand show consistent performance regardless of the added delay.

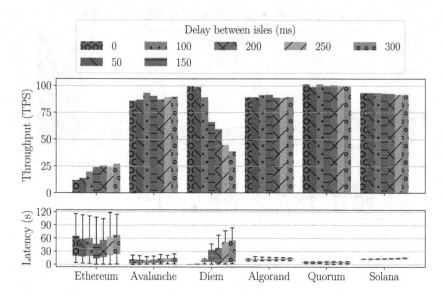

Fig. 8. Throughput and latency, 100 TPS workload, varied delay between the isles

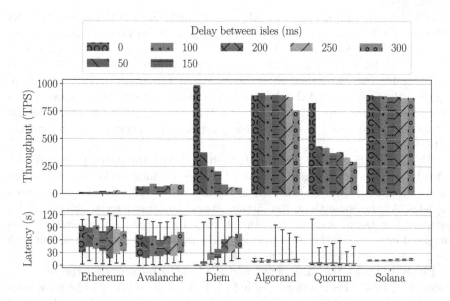

Fig. 9. Throughput and latency, 1,000 TPS workload, varied delay between the isles

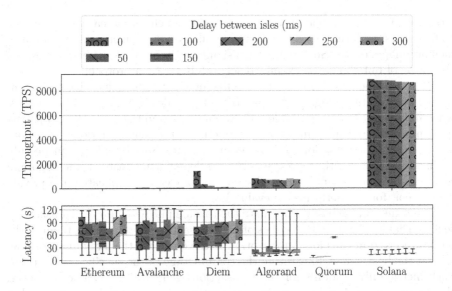

Fig. 10. Throughput and latency, 10,000 TPS workload, varied delay between the isles

For the comparison of the results of the evaluation in AWS and iLab environments, we use the results presented in [12]. The corresponding results are displayed in Fig. 9. As we see in both figures, for the low-latency setups, as `datacenter` or `testnet`, Diem reaches its maximum throughput given the provided workload. On the other hand, when we increase the latency between the nodes and use geographically distributed regions as in `devnet` or `community`, we observe a significant drop in the throughput of Diem. The results correspond to the experiments with the increased latency in the iLab environment. As for the other blockchains, such as Algorand or Solana, they are optimized for the public networks and increased latencies, and therefore we don't see the drop in throughput, as shown in the figures for AWS and iLab environments.

4 Discussion

In this section, we look at the different aspects of the evaluation which can be taken into account in order to increase the depth of understanding of the blockchain protocols. While we performed an extensive set of tests in various environments, there are still more factors and variables that can be changed and which can affect the performance of the protocols.

The work was focused on the behavior of the blockchain protocols under different network conditions, the experiments were limited to the network sizes up to 35 blockchain nodes. Even on smaller scale with emulated delays, we were able to capture similar performance trends to the geo-distributed settings.

We performed the experiments using the default system configurations supplied by the image provider. However, blockchain protocols like Solana recommend[1] different operating system tuning, such as increasing the size of UDP buffers, as Solana uses UDP for communication, or increasing the limit of memory mapped files. Such tweaks can significantly improve the performance of the protocol but should be examined separately for each protocol.

Protocols such as Algorand have different node types which have different modes of operation. Algorand separates relay nodes and participation nodes, where relay nodes are responsible for communication in the network, and participation nodes participate in consensus. In our deployment scenario, we ran both a relay and a participation node on each machine. Such topology can be suboptimal and not exactly represent a typical deployment. Instead, the Algorand main network can be analyzed, and such topology can be replicated in a private deployment for the performance evaluation.

In our measurements, we calculate the throughput based on the transactions sent by Diablo. We store the hashes of the transactions and compare them to the hashes received in the block subscription or the query for the individual transaction. If the hashes match, we store the commit time of the specific transactions. Such metric only accounts for the transactions generated by Diablo. However, the Solana protocol includes voting transactions into the blocks, meaning that the calculated throughput can be higher if those transactions are included.

Another important point is that while we used the dynamic fee interface for Avalanche, we still observed that some transactions were dropped due to the insufficient fees specified in the transactions. There are multiple possible approaches to solve this issue. On the one hand, we tried to calculate the transaction fees online during the experiment run using the data provided by the blockchain network. It is possible that the approach was not perfect, and therefore the calculation logic can be reviewed and improved. On the other hand, it might be possible to specify static fees in the Avalanche configuration so that they do not provide overhead for the experiment, allowing only to benchmark the raw transaction processing performance. Also, while we experimented with C-Chain, it is important to measure the performance of X-Chain as well.

The differences in the cloud environment and the lab testbed do not allow strict comparison of the metrics. Due to the hardware differences, we can only look at the tendencies and the order of change, but not the exact numbers.

5   Related Work

Dinh et al. [7] showcase Blockbench, a benchmarking framework designed with the focus on permissioned blockchains. They use a commodity cluster of 48 machines interconnected with a gigabit switch. In the experiments, the number of blockchain nodes is varied from 1 to 32.

Saingre et al. [20] use two clusters with Raspberry Pi machines and an HPC-grade cluster. Two network sizes are mentioned without the deployment specification regarding virtualization, containerization, and blockchain node

---

[1] https://docs.solana.com/running-validator/validator-start#linux.

distribution across the physical machines. The used versions of blockchain protocols are not specified as well.

Chacko et al. [3] introduce HyperLedgerLab, a benchmarking framework for Hyperledger Fabric. The authors use a Kubernetes cluster consisting of several task-specific nodes. Two cluster setups used for experiments consist of 3 worker nodes which run the Fabric components, and 32 worker nodes respectively. In one of the experiments, the authors introduce an additional network delay of 90 to 110 milliseconds to emulate a geographically distributed environment, and note a negative impact on the performance of the Fabric network.

Nasrulin et al. [14] propose Gromit. They used a cluster of four servers in a single datacenter. The blockchain network sizes from 4 to 128 are mentioned without specifying whether any virtualization or containerization was used, and without mentioning the distribution of blockchain nodes across the four servers. Emulation of geo-distributed setting is present in one of the experiments without specifying the exact configuration of the network emulator. Considering that multiple blockchain nodes are deployed on a single machine as different processes, only filtering by network destination port is possible. This fact leads to the lack of clarity regarding the replication of network delays between the cities, as pings between different pairs of nodes might be different.

In [18], Ren et al. run the experiments on a single machine, with three network sizes of 4, 8, and 16 nodes. The authors point out the limitation of creating a large-scale blockchain network on a single machine. It is also reported that Quorum failed to commit transactions with empty smart contract calls given a workload of 500 TPS and a network size of 8 and 16.

Chervinski et al. [5] run their experiments on a network of 5 commodity machines. The authors emulate the ping time of 200 ms between the machines. The number of validators for each of two blockchain protocols varies from 5 to 128, distributed across the machines.

Chacko et al. [2] outline the need for benchmarking each blockchain in the most suited setup specified in the documentation of this blockchain. This often contradicts with comparing different blockchains on the same ground [12]: instead of fine-tuning specific setup for each blockchain one must typically choose the same setup, as realistic as possible, for all blockchains.

Some evaluations compared blockchains on ad hoc benchmarks. Han et al. [13] focused on comparing Ripple, Tendermint, Corda and Hyperledger Fabric to evaluate their scalability potential in the context of Internet of Things. They used the Emulab environment and configured network resources with ns-3. Shapiro et al. [21] compared the performance of blockchains relying exclusively on Byzantine fault tolerant consensus protocols, namely Burrow, Quorum and Redbelly Blockchain [22], on AWS.

While local clusters and emulated network delays were used in prior work, we use Diablo [12] to execute the same set of experiments as in the geo-distributed environment, and allow the comparison of the performance trends of the six state-of-the-art blockchain protocols. Furthermore, we show that tail latency provides additional insight to the impact of underlying protocol implementation and details, such as consensus algorithm.

6   Conclusion

Our study explored the benefits and drawbacks of cloud environments and local bare metal clusters. Our findings indicated that switches within the LAN had minimal impact on blockchain performance. Additionally, we demonstrated that the average transaction latency of blockchains often failed to accurately represent their tail latency. Notably, the performance patterns observed on our cluster, which incorporated artificial network delays, showed the same behavior as those obtained in geo-distributed settings.

As future work, we plan to evaluate the Redbelly Blockchain [22] on bare metal as it has already been integrated to Diablo [12] and showed superior performance than the blockchains we evaluated here.

Acknowledgements. The authors wish to thank Georg Carle, Holger Kinkelin, Filip Rezabek for their feedback on ealier versions of this paper. This work is supported in part by the Australian Research Council Future Fellowship funding scheme (#180100496).

References

1. Bano, S., et al.: State machine replication in the libra blockchain (2019). https://developers.libra.org/docs/assets/papers/libra-consensus-state-machine-replication--the-libra-blockchain.pdf, Accessed 01 Oct 2019
2. Chacko, J.A., Mayer, R., Fekete, A., Gramoli, V., Jacobsen, H.A.: How to benchmark permissioned blockchains. In: 15th TPC Technology Conference on Performance Evaluation & Benchmarking (TPCTC 2023) (2023)
3. Chacko, J.A., Mayer, R., Jacobsen, H.A.: Why do my blockchain transactions fail?: A Study of hyperledger fabric. In: Proceedings of the 2021 International Conference on Management of Data, pp. 221–234. ACM, Virtual Event China, June 2021. https://doi.org/10.1145/3448016.3452823, https://dl.acm.org/doi/10.1145/3448016.3452823
4. Chase, J.: Quorum whitepaper (2019). https://github.com/ConsenSys/quorum/blob/master/docs/Quorum%20Whitepaper%20v0.2.pdf, Accessed 04 Dec 2020
5. Chervinski, J.O., Kreutz, D., Xu, X., Yu, J.: Analyzing the performance of the inter-blockchain communication protocol. In: 2023 53rd Annual IEEE/IFIP International Conference on Dependable Systems and Networks (DSN), pp. 151–164. IEEE, Porto, Portugal, June 2023. https://doi.org/10.1109/DSN58367.2023.00026, https://ieeexplore.ieee.org/document/10202634/
6. Dean, J., Barroso, L.A.: The tail at scale. Commun. ACM **56**(2), 74–80 (2013). https://doi.org/10.1145/2408776.2408794, https://dl.acm.org/doi/10.1145/2408776.2408794
7. Dinh, T.T.A., Wang, J., Chen, G., Liu, R., Ooi, B.C., Tan, K.L.: Blockbench: a framework for analyzing private blockchains. In: Proceedings of the 2017 ACM International Conference on Management of Data, pp. 1085–1100 (2017)

8. Fan, C., Ghaemi, S., Khazaei, H., Musilek, P.: Performance evaluation of blockchain systems: a systematic survey. IEEE Access **8**, 126927–126950 (2020). https://doi.org/10.1109/ACCESS.2020.3006078, https://ieeexplore.ieee.org/document/9129732/
9. Gallenmüller*, S., Scholz*, D., Stubbe, H., Carle, G.: The POS Framework: a methodology and toolchain for reproducible network experiments. In: The 17th International Conference on Emerging Networking Experiments and Technologies (CoNEXT 2021). Munich, Germany (Virtual Event), December 2021. https://doi.org/10.1145/3485983.3494841
10. Gilad, Y., Hemo, R., Micali, S., Vlachos, G., Zeldovich, N.: Algorand: scaling byzantine agreements for cryptocurrencies. In: Proceedings of the 26th Symposium on Operating Systems Principles, pp. 51–68 (2017)
11. Gramoli, V., Guerraoui, R., Lebedev, A., Natoli, C., Voron, G.: Diablo: a benchmark suite for blockchains, October 2022. https://doi.org/10.5281/zenodo.7707312, https://doi.org/10.5281/zenodo.7707312
12. Gramoli, V., Guerraoui, R., Lebedev, A., Natoli, C., Voron, G.: Diablo: a benchmark suite for blockchains. In: Proceedings of the Eighteenth European Conference on Computer Systems, pp. 540–556. ACM, Rome Italy, May 2023. https://doi.org/10.1145/3552326.3567482, https://dl.acm.org/doi/10.1145/3552326.3567482
13. Han, R., Shapiro, G., Gramoli, V., Xu, X.: On the performance of distributed ledgers for internet of things. Internet Things **10**, 100087 (2020)
14. Nasrulin, B., De Vos, M., Ishmaev, G., Pouwelse, J.: Gromit: benchmarking the performance and scalability of blockchain systems. In: 2022 IEEE International Conference on Decentralized Applications and Infrastructures (DAPPS), pp. 56–63. IEEE, Newark, CA, USA, August 2022. https://doi.org/10.1109/DAPPS55202.2022.00015, https://ieeexplore.ieee.org/document/9899852/
15. Natoli, C., Yu, J., Gramoli, V., Veríssimo, P.J.E.: Deconstructing blockchains: a comprehensive survey on consensus, membership and structure. Technical Report, 1908.08316, arXiv (2019), http://arxiv.org/abs/1908.08316
16. Pahl, M.O.: The iLab concept: making teaching better, at scale. IEEE Commun. Mag. **55**(11), 178–185 (2017). https://doi.org/10.1109/MCOM.2017.1700394, http://ieeexplore.ieee.org/xpl/articleDetails.jsp?tp=&arnumber=8114571&contentType=Journals+Magazines
17. Ranchal-Pedrosa, A., Gramoli, V.: Zlb, a blockchain tolerating colluding majorities (2023)
18. Ren, K., et al.: BBSF: blockchain benchmarking standardized framework. In: Proceedings of the 1st Workshop on Verifiable Database Systems, pp. 10–18. ACM, Seattle WA USA, June 2023. https://doi.org/10.1145/3595647.3595649, https://dl.acm.org/doi/10.1145/3595647.3595649
19. Rocket, T.: Snowflake to avalanche: a novel metastable consensus protocol family for cryptocurrencies. Technical Report (2018). https://ipfs.io/ipfs/QmUy4jh5mGNZvLkjies1RWM4YuvJh5o2FYopNPVYwrRVGV, Accessed 26 Nov 2021
20. Saingre, D., Ledoux, T., Menaud, J.M.: BCTMark: a Framework for benchmarking blockchain technologies. In: 2020 IEEE/ACS 17th International Conference on Computer Systems and Applications (AICCSA), pp. 1–8. IEEE, Antalya, Turkey, November 2020. https://doi.org/10.1109/AICCSA50499.2020.9316536, https://ieeexplore.ieee.org/document/9316536/
21. Shapiro, G., Natoli, C., Gramoli, V.: The performance of byzantine fault tolerant blockchains. In: Proceedings of the 19th IEEE International Symposium on Network Computing and Applications (NCA 2020), pp. 1–8, November 2020

22. Tennakoon, D., Hua, Y., Gramoli, V.: Smart redbelly blockchain: reducing congestion for web3. In: IEEE International Parallel and Distributed Processing Symposium, IPDPS, pp. 940–950. IEEE (2023)

23. Touloupou, M., Themistocleous, M., Iosif, E., Christodoulou, K.: A systematic literature review toward a blockchain benchmarking framework. IEEE Access **10**, 70630–70644 (2022). https://doi.org/10.1109/ACCESS.2022.3188123, https://ieeexplore.ieee.org/document/9813702/

24. Wang, X., Duan, S., Clavin, J., Zhang, H.: BFT in blockchains: from protocols to use cases. ACM Comput. Surv. **54**(10s), 1–37 (2022). https://doi.org/10.1145/3503042, https://dl.acm.org/doi/10.1145/3503042

25. Wood, G.: Ethereum: a secure decentralised generalised transaction ledger (2015), yellow paper

26. Yakovenko, A.: Solana: a new architecture for a high performance blockchain v0.8.13 (2021). https://solana.com/solana-whitepaper.pdf, Accessed 26 Dec 2021

EVM-Vale: Formal Verification of EVM Bytecode Using Vale

Daniel Cumming[1] , Mark Utting[1]([✉]) , Franck Cassez[2] , Naipeng Dong[1] ,
Sadra Bayat Tork[1], and Marten Risius[3]

[1] School of Electrical Engineering and Computer Science, University of Queensland,
Brisbane, Australia
m.utting@uq.edu.au
[2] Windranger Labs, Sydney, NSW, Australia
[3] School of Business, University of Queensland, Brisbane, Australia

Abstract. We evaluate the use of the existing Microsoft Vale framework to guarantee correctness of low level Ethereum Virtual Machine (EVM) bytecode, while affording smart contract developers higher-level language and reasoning features. We encode EVM-R (a subset of EVM semantics and instruction set) into F*, and raise the EVM-R into Vale design-by-contract components in an intermediate language supporting conditional logic. The specifications of Vale procedures constructed from these verified EVM bytecodes carry integrity to the bytecode level, unlike current EVM compilers. Furthermore, raising the instruction set to Vale allows opportunity for refinement of the instructions, which we did ensuring safety properties of overflow protection, invalid memory access protection, and functional correctness. We demonstrate our contributions through two case study smart contracts, a simple casino, and a subcurrency coin.

Keywords: Ethereum · EVM · Vale · formal methods · software verification · smart contracts

1 Introduction

Since Satoshi Nakamoto's 2008 paper, blockchain and crypto-currency technology has been increasing in development and adoption. Many instantiations of blockchain technology have occurred, however this paper is concerned with blockchains that have two key attributes: all transactions are recorded on a publicly viewable ledger, and there is an immutable history of entries into that ledger. The distrubuted network of a blockchain can handle more than standard currency transactions, blockchains can store programs or 'smart contracts' which can execute complex code, initiated from a transaction.

Supported by Cyber Research Seed Funding, Cyber Security Centre, UQ.

Since Ethereum's creation, more than 200 million smart contracts [9] have been deployed on the Ethereum network, including around 760 thousand ERC-20 smart contracts managing more than USD$260 billion at time of writing [10]. This makes smart contracts a prime target for hackers to exploit for financial gain. Unfortunately, all smart contracts deployed are particularly susceptible to exploitation, since their code is posted to the publicly viewable ledger for everyone to see, and the code is immutable once deployed. This means that bugs in a smart contract can have devastating consequences, with smart contract bugs regularly losing companies and users millions of dollars worth of cryptocurrency [20].

Fortunately, there are options developers can take to protect their code from exploitation. There are many tools available to developers to assist with testing, analysis, and formal verification of their code before it is deployed. Formal verification of code offers the highest-level of assurance that code is bug-free. Programs that have been formally verified mathematically prove that the code contains no bugs, relative to a developer defined specification[1]. Many tools available for Ethereum smart contract verification work on Solidity source code, and while this can offer a high level of assurance, the compiled binary is still vulnerable to bugs introduced by the compiler. In order for the binary to be formally verified, one of two options must be followed: either verify the Solidity compiler against a formalism of Solidity, or verify the EVM binary post-compilation against an EVM program specification. Currently there is no official formal semantics for Solidity, although there have been attempts and progress made [16,17,23]. However verifying an entire compiler is an enormous task, and the Solidity compiler is regularly updated, whereas EVM bytecode is more stable and formalised [15,22]. For these reasons we are focusing on the second option.

There have been previous projects that provide methods of verifying EVM Bytecode programs [5,13,15], however our approach differs as we utilize the Microsoft Research tool Vale. In this paper we will explore the usefulness of Vale as a tool to verify Ethereum smart contracts. We chose Vale as it allows us the *unique* ability to skip the compilation of the source language entirely, and develop verifiable higher-level programs by building from bytecode up. By exploring the usefulness of Vale as a tool to verify Etherum smart contracts, we make four key contributions:

1. We show that Vale can be used to verify simple Ethereum smart contracts at the EVM level, without any changes to Vale.
2. We successfully encode a significant subset of the EVM bytecode into Vale, thus demonstrating that Vale can support EVM semantics.
3. We find that the current state of the Vale/F* tooling is sufficient for small case studies, but seems to have significant problem scaling up to larger procedures. This makes it a less competitive option compared to other EVM bytecode verification tools.

---

[1] This is a subtle point for those unfamiliar with formal methods, but an important one. If a specification the developer verifies against is *incorrect*, then the proof they have is at best a correct proof for an incorrect specification.

4. We identify several improvements to Vale and its interaction with F* that would help to make it more usable for smart contract verification.

Section 2 introduces the EVM, F* and VALE. Section 3 outlines our formalization of a subset of the EVM instructions in F* and VALE. Section 4 describes two case studies and Sect. 5 discusses the challenges faced, then Sect. 6 discusses related work and Sect. 7 gives our conclusions.

2   Background

2.1   The Ethereum Virtual Machine

Ethereum is able to record smart contracts on the blockchain that are able to be executed via transactions. This means that Ethereum is more than just a distributed ledger, it is a distributed state machine where transactions initiate state transitions. This distributed state machine tracks the current state of all accounts globally, where each account is either an externally owned account or a contract account. Each account can store a balance of Ether, however only externally owned accounts can initialise transactions, and only contract accounts can store program code and data persistently on the blockchain (in storage).

When a contract account receives a transaction from an externally owned account, the program code can be executed, and the effects after successful execution are updated in the global state. The code is executed via a virtual machine known as The Ethereum Virtual Machine (referred to as EVM from now on), which is a stack machine architecture where the stack contains a maximum of 1024 integers of size 256 bits. EVM smart contracts also have access to local memory which is not persistent, and they are able to read and write to storage which is persistent. The opcodes that form the language of EVM are described by the Ethereum Foundation in the Yellow Paper, but are more accurately and formally detailed by Hildebrandt *et al.* in KEVM, and the small-step semantics of Grischenko, Maffei, and Schneidewind [13].

2.2   FStar

FStar (commonly stylised F*)[2] is an effectful functional programming language whose purpose is program verification. It is developed and maintained by Microsoft and Inria. F* is able to be used as an interactive and automated theorem prover that uses the SMT solver Z3 to discharge verification conditions, such as strong typing conditions, data structure invariants, proofs that functions terminate and so on. F* programs are not directly executable and must be translated to either F# or OCaml to produce an executable binary.

---

[2] F* documentation and resources are available at: https://www.fstar-lang.org.

2.3   Vale

VALE is an open source Microsoft research tool and language[3] for the development of verified assembly-language programs, typically used to verify high-performance cryptographic algorithms written in x64 assembler. Vale operates in conjunction with an underlying verification framework, currently Dafny and F* are supported.

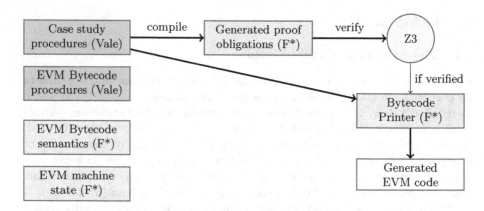

Fig. 1. The smart contract verification process using Vale. The bottom two F* layers on the left define the EVM machine and bytecode semantics, then the Vale layer above defines the EVM bytecode instructions as Vale procedures - these layers are reusable for all case studies. The top Vale layer defines the smart contract procedures for the current case study, which are translated by Vale into verification proof conditions then verified using Z3. If verification is successful, then the Printer can be run to extract executable EVM bytecode from each case study procedure.

As shown in Fig. 1, a Vale project firstly requires the semantics and instruction set of the target assembly language to be encoded in F* or Dafny. This amounts to writing a denotational semantics for the instruction set, to define how each instruction transforms the state of the system into a new state.

Secondly, the semantic definitions of that instruction set are then raised up into the Vale language level by defining one or more imperative procedures in the Vale language, corresponding to each assembly instruction. These procedures have an axiomatic semantics with **requires/ensures** specifications that define how the system state is updated when each instruction is invoked. The Vale system uses Hoare logic reasoning to automatically verify that the semantics of each of these imperative procedures correctly matches the semantics of the corresponding instruction in the denotational semantics defined earlier. One advantage of this two-layered approach is that it is possible to define multiple procedures giving different views of a single assembler instruction, ranging from

---

[3] Vale is available on GitHub: https://github.com/project-everest/vale under an Apache 2.0 license.

simple usage to more complex usage with stronger preconditions and postconditions, but more reasoning overhead. This allows developers to choose the most appropriate view of each instruction for their application, and to use the stronger views only when they are needed, as we shall discuss in Sect. 3.1.

The third step in using Vale is to write higher-level imperative procedures that combine multiple assembler instructions into reusable blocks, which are then verified against the individual assembler instructions in the body of the procedure. These higher-level procedures can contain **if-else** statements and **while** loops to support structured programming - Vale translates these control-flow constructs into lower-level jumps and labels when the final assembly code is generated for the whole system. This gradual layering of higher-level procedures allows more complex procedures and algorithms to be expressed in a natural style. In this way, developers can specify entire programs using the Vale language and raised procedures, which are then automatically verified for correctness. To verify a program, Vale translates the program into the same verification framework the semantics were encoded in. The translated program is then verified using that framework. Since the output of the Vale is verified by the underlying framework, Vale does not need to form part of the trusted computing base, or be verified itself.

Once an assembly language semantics and instruction set is specified in the underlying framework, developers that wish to verify programs in that assembly language do not need to interact directly with that semantics, they should only need to interact with Vale as input (although in practice sometimes extra lemmas must be added into the semantics level). However, since the program verification is performed on the translated program, in the underlying framework, verification *errors* are expressed in terms of the translated program with no reference to the Vale source code. This has the disadvantage that developers may need to be familiar with the underlying framework to interpret those errors.

3 Encoding EVM-R into F* and Raising into Vale

We aim to explore whether Vale (without modification) is a suitable tool for the verification of EVM bytecode, taking into account the Vale features that give developers access to some higher-level language constructs that support structured code. To be suitable as a verification tool for EVM bytecode, Vale will need to provide the ability to specify and implement smart contracts in a clear and brief manner, the verification will need to be automatic (or close to), and verified programs will need to be runnable on the EVM. In order to determine the utility of Vale for our goal, we do not need to encode the complete semantics of EVM into F*[4], since a restricted subset is sufficient and is simpler to implement. We instead encode a restricted subset of EVM, referred to as **EVM-R**, that will contain no *extra* functionality to EVM, only simplifications and restrictions.

---

[4] We have chosen F* as the underlying verification framework that Vale will interact with since it has a measurable performance increase over Dafny [11].

The inclusions and exclusions of EVM-R are determined by what is necessary to verify the functional correctness of the two case studies 4, with the assumption that sufficient gas is provided. Both case studies require logical and arithmetic operations, reads and writes to memory and storage, some information from the calling context (e.g. the block timestamp from the transaction state), balance tracking and transfers, valid and invalid end of execution with and without return data, conditional branching, and appropriate errors for stack and integer over-and-underflows, reads to uninitialised memory, and transfers with insufficient balance.

We retrict EVM-R to have no inter-contract calls, no model for non-caller storage, no gas model, simplified integers[5], simplified account creation, keccak crypographic hashing and logging functions are simplified to blackbox deterministic functions, and loops are not supported. A summary of the inclusions and exclusions can be read from 1. All of these restrictions could be removed given time, but are not a problem for our current case studies and goal.

Table 1. The features of EVM that EVM-R supports, and what it omits

Supported	Restricted
Logical and arithmetic operations	No external or inter-contract calls
Read and write to caller storage	No tracking of non-caller storage
Read and write to local memory	Gas model is omitted
Query required calling context	All integers natural numbers $< 2^{256}$
Balance tracking and transfers	Simplified account creation
End of execution and return data	Simplify keccak to opaque deterministic
Conditional branching	Loops are not supported
Stack overflow protection	
Integer overflow protection	
Uninitialised memory protection	
Insufficient balance errors	

EVM-R is modelled by a simplified EVM state as shown in Fig. 2. Instructions are defined as state transitions, where the next state is an update of the previous state subject to the semantics of the instruction and the EVM global rules. If the processing of an instruction breaks the global EVM rules, such as stack overflow or underflow, then an exception state is triggered which invalidates verification by setting the ok flag in the state to false. All other end states are permissible, and do not invalidate verification. Note that the status value in

---

[5] nat256 bounded natural integers ($\forall\, i \in$ nat256 $: i \in \mathbb{Z} \land 0 \leq i < 2^{256}$), and therefore we currently do not support negative numbers, bitwise operations, or bytes. Without bytes, PUSH1...PUSH32 instructions are simplified to one PUSH instruction and memory is a contiguous array of nat256 integers instead of bytes.

```
type state = {
    ok: bool; // True if verification successful, false if unsucessfull
    status: execStatus; // Execution status (e.g. ACTIVE)
    stack: (s:Seq.seq nat256 {0 <= Seq.length s && Seq.length s < 1024});
    mem: (Seq.seq nat256); // Memory of this account
    stor: (Map.t nat256 nat256); // Storage of this account
    bal: (Map.t address nat256); // Balances of all accounts
    ...
}

let eval_ins (s:state) (i:Instruction) : state =
    match i with
        | Add ->
            v0 <-- pop s.stack;
            v1 <-- pop s.stack;
            push ((v0 + v1) % pow2_256) s.stack
        | ...
```

Fig. 2. Simplified snippets of the F* encoding of the EVM-R state, and an example of the state transformation that occurs from the Add instruction

the state models the result status of the bytecode execution, and can be ACTIVE for on-going execution, END_INVALID after executing the Invalid bytecode, or END_SELFDESTRUCT after executing the Selfdestruct bytecode, etc. The second half of Fig. 2 shows the *eval_ins* function that computes the state transition for instructions, with **Add** as an example.

The successful encoding of EVM-R in F* allows the targeted bytecode instructions to be raised to the Vale level into 'design-by-contract' components [18] featuring preconditions, postconditions, and access modifiers. The body of the raised Vale components is empty, as the implementation refers to the semantics of the instruction encoded in the underlying verification framework, this can be seen in Fig. 3 by the :instruction attribute labelled A. that references the relevant instruction in the F* Semantics module.

3.1 Handling Arithmetic Overflow via Refinement

There is some flexibility in designing the specifications of raised-instruction components, provided that the underlying instruction implementation is a correct refinement [7,19] of each specification. It is possible to write several alternative raised component views of the same instruction, some with more restrictive specifications that give stronger properties, such as guaranteeing freedom from arithmetic overflow. For example, the underlying EVM-R **Add** instruction does arithmetic modulo 256 bits, but we provide two raised components that give different views of this instruction:

- **ADD_WRAP**[6] follows the EVM semantics closely, wrapping modulo 2^{256};
- **ADD** is a *restricted* view of the underlying EVM semantics, with a stronger precondition that restricts the input arguments to ensure they will not overflow. This allows this **ADD** component to have a simpler postcondition that just adds the top two elements of the stack using standard (unbounded) mathematical addition, which is much easier for SMT solvers to reason about than modulo arithmetic.

Note that when a developer uses the restricted **ADD** specification in a smart contract, the generated proof obligations guarantee that overflow is impossible, otherwise verification will be unsuccessful as the precondition is violated. Since **ADD** and **ADD_WRAP** are both refined by the underlying EVM-R **Add** instruction (this is verified when Fig. 3 is processed by VALE), they can be replaced with the underlying EVM-R **Add** instruction during printing, with correctness preserved. Verifying freedom from overflow statically like this is usually far preferable to allowing overflow to happen at runtime, which results in more complex EVM bytecode with exceptions or conditionals, and increased gas charges.

Our Vale version of EVM-R provides restricted (non-wrapping) instructions that guarantee overflow protection for all wrapping arithmetic in the EVM instruction set. Similarly, we provide restricted memory-reading instructions that guarantee that every memory access is to initialised memory. We also provide a library called SafeMath with `SafeAdd` and `SafeSub` procedures which first perform a dynamic check on the arguments of Add and Sub that will revert if integer overflow or underflow would occur, before then calling the refined **ADD** or `SUB` instruction. This is needed when addition or subtraction is performed on unbounded data, which may come from a storage read or from call data. SafeMath demonstrates the ability for Vale procedures to be constructed to allow portability of common patterns, with verification of their correctness.

3.2 Unimplemented Features

A key feature that was unable to be fully implemented (see Sect. 5 for details) is printing the smart contract bytecode out as a runnable EVM binary after the verification of a smart contract succeeds. The printer needs to convert the Vale source code into a valid EVM bytecode program, calculating the program counter and converting the 'if' statements within procedures into **JUMPI** and **JUMPDEST** instructions, and all instructions converted to their relevant instruction value (e.g. **ADD** → 0x01).

4 Case Studies

The code for this EVM-Vale project and the case studies can be found in our GitHub repository https://github.com/uqcyber/VeriSmart.git. Code snippets presented in figures within this paper are simplified and may not parse if copied into a Vale project.

---

[6] The name **ADD_WRAP** was chosen as this is consistent with other Vale projects.

```
procedure ADD()
  {:public}
  {:instruction Instruction(Semantics.Add)} // A.
  reads
    status;
  modifies
    stack;
  requires
    status == ACTIVE ==> 1 < length(stack);
    status == ACTIVE ==> stack[0] + stack[1] < pow2_256; // B.
  ensures
    old(status) == ACTIVE ==> (
      stack == old(stack[1..][0 := stack[0] + stack[1]]));
    inactive_state_unchanged(old(this), this);
{
}

procedure ADD_WRAP()
  {:public}
  {:instruction Instruction(Semantics.Add)} // A.
  reads
    status;
  modifies
    stack;
  requires
    status == ACTIVE ==> 1 < length(stack);
  ensures
    old(status) == ACTIVE ==> (
      stack == old(stack[1..][0 := (stack[0] + stack[1]) % pow2_256]));
    inactive_state_unchanged(old(this), this);
{
}
```

Fig. 3. Vale procedures **ADD** and **ADD_WRAP**. **ADD** is a restricted version of the EVM Add instruction with a stronger precondition preventing overflow. **ADD_WRAP** is consistent with the EVM Add instruction and wraps modulo 2^{256}.

4.1 Casino

This case study is motivated by Ahrendt *et al.*'s [1] Solidity smart contract for a simple casino. Ahrendt *et al.* verified functional correctness of several functions of the smart contract at the Solidity level. We implement the same contract as EVM bytecode, and verify functional correctness of all functions of the contract as well as demonstrate that we guarantee freedom from integer overflow and invalid memory accesses.

All functions maintain a global invariant over the life of the smart contract. This invariant includes the predicates that are listed in comments in the Solidity casino file, as well as some properties that are required for verification of the full contract. For example, one of the invariants from the Solidity contract maintains that the contract's balance is always the sum of the pot and the wager, and another one ensures that the wager is zero if and only if there is no active game. Other invariant properties reflect rules of EVM architecture, such as the relationship of key addresses e.g. `actor != sender` (Fig. 4).

We replicate the same contract variables as the Solidity contract, except at the Vale level we do not have enum types for `State` and `Coin`, nor struct types for `Wager`. For the `State` variable, there is a predicate added to the invariant that maintains that `State` is always either 0 for IDLE, 1 for GAME_AVAILABLE, or 2 for BET_PLACED. The `Coin` has HEADS and TAILS implemented as odd or even integers, and all inputs for the coin flip are modulo 2. Instead of implementing `Wager` as a struct, we expand it and explicitly store each member of the struct in a different location in storage. Storage variables are accessed by their indexes, but for each storage variable we define a constant with a meaningful name to use as the index. For example, the state of the casino is stored at position 0, therefore it can be accessed by `stor[casino_state]`, where the constant `casino_state` is defined to be zero.

Modifiers in the Solidity contract check various common properties. We implement each modifier as a Vale procedure that uses conditional logic. If the modifier property is satisfied then the procedure returns with the execution status as ACTIVE and the modifier property is included in the postcondition. If the property is not satisfied then the procedure calls REVERT or INVALID which ends execution. Aside from the modifiers in the Solidity contract, we developed some extra modifiers that help to maintain particular properties, such as `validCallValue` which checks that the call value provided is in an acceptable range. We removed the original `costs` modifier entirely — it was used to check that a function input argument called `_value` was the same as the call value. Instead we opted to use the call value directly as there is no reason to have this duplicate input argument.

In Solidity, one can mark a function as payable, this indicates that Ether can be added as call value to the transaction from the transactor's account, to be deposited to the actor's account. The transfer of Ether in this way is handled externally to the EVM, and so we implemented a `payable` procedure that assumes that the transfer of balances occurs, as there are no bytecode instructions to facilitate this.

All functions from the Solidity contract are implemented by defining smaller helper procedures that group sequences of bytecode together into logical and reusable segments that are easy to understand and use. This use of modularity is preferable to writing the functions directly in bytecode, which would create long bytecode sequences that are difficult to understand. Each function has particular properties that must be true for successful execution, these are a combination of the modifiers and properties that ensure the EVM does not reach an invalid state e.g. stack overflow. We implemented 'safe' versions of each function that implements the behaviour executed by the function, and includes all properties required for valid execution in the precondition. These safe functions are then wrapped in a function with the target Solidity function name, this function must establish the precondition of the safe function prior to the safe function call.

Many of the procedures are large and required some help to be given to the SMT solver for consistent verification. This help included providing **assert** statements throughout the implementation; increasing the F* SMT solver settings (fuel, ifuel, and rlimit) to large values; restarting the verifier; or separating procedures into separate files.

All functions from the Solidity contract are implemented, specified, verified, and also verifiably maintain our desired safety properties of protection from integer overflow and uninitialised memory access.

```
1   old(status) == ACTIVE ==> (
2       (stor[casino_state] == bet_placed ==> stor[wager_value] <= stor[pot]) &&
3       stor[wager_timestamp] <= timeStamp &&
4       actor != sender &&
5       actor != stor[operator_address] &&
6       actor != stor[player_address] &&
7       (stor[casino_state] == bet_placed ==>
8           stor[pot] + stor[wager_value] == bal[actor]) &&
9       (stor[casino_state] != bet_placed ==> stor[pot] == bal[actor])
10  );
```

Fig. 4. Casino contract invariant.

The Casino smart contract took 1771 non-comment lines of Vale code to specify and verify, including 24 procedures that contained a total of 1234 lines of specification and 222 lines of code in the procedure bodies. This is a very high ratio (5.6:1) of specification to code, and we would like to develop patterns and idioms for reducing this specification overhead in future. Roughly one third of the lines of executable code (73/222) were EVM bytecode instructions, while the other two thirds were calls to helper procedures, **if-else** control-flow statements and **assert** statements etc.

4.2   Coin

Implementing and specifying the example **Coin** smart contract from the Solidity language documentation [8] in EVM-Vale was similar to the Casino, except simpler. The Solidity smart contract for Coin saves a mapping of addresses to balances of the subcurrency. Much like the structs in the casino, the keys of this mapping are stored directly, however they are shifted by an offset so that the other contract variables are at the start of storage. Therefore the balance of address 42 is accessed by `stor[42 + offset]`. This is sufficient to verify toy examples with small addresses, but to support arbitrary 160 bit addresses in future we will need a more accurate model of the Ethereum storage trie, which maps addresses to values.

The Coin smart contract took 331 non-comment lines of Vale code to specify and verify, including six procedures that contained a total of 147 lines of specification and 70 lines of code in the procedure bodies, of which 33 were EVM bytecode instructions. This is still a high ratio (2:1) of specification to code, but about half the specification lines are just listing variables in **reads** and **modifies**, so if we discount those then the number of specification and code lines is roughly equal, which is a reasonable specification overhead.

5   Challenges

We encountered particular challenges at different stages in the process of encoding EVM into Vale. Some of these we have resolved, and some are still outstanding issues. Vale comes with limited documentation, but since it is open source, a lot can be learned by looking under the hood, and Microsoft researchers offer some support for persistent difficulties via the Project Everest Slack channels.

Type Restrictions: We found the Vale type system to be restrictive and difficult to understand, often with information only being gained by following the typechecker in the source code. The biggest difficulty this presented was that the guards of **if** and **while** statements must contain either a binary operation between types that can be coerced to integers, or 'operand_type's. The documentation for 'operand_type's is perhaps the most lacking and their implementation requirements the most obscure, and once implemented we found their behaviour with the verifier to be unintuitive and difficult.

In order to have access to the top of the stack as a branching condition for conditional logic, we instead implemented a simple hack where we added a 'virtual' natural number field into the state to represent if the head of the stack was zero or not. This member of the state is never actually written, and when referencing this in Vale, the underlying F* is redirected to a function that evaluates the condition based on the stack at the time. A natural number was not the first choice for this value, but initial implementation with a boolean uncovered that guards in Vale must be binary comparisons between integer values.

Further problems with the Vale type system were that constants are unable to be referenced in all contexts, this meant that we had to duplicate definitions of constants with shadow definitions that would pass the typechecker. Consider the constant `player_address` and shadow constant `player_address'` from the Casino case study. Both constants are needed as the first can be used only in the implementation, and the second can be used only in the specification. This becomes a code maintenance issue as there is no actual link between the two constants.

Most if not all of these difficulties could likely be avoided by modifying the Vale system to support more flexible syntax and types. Since Vale does not form part of the trusted computing base, this would not affect the soundness of the verification. However, for our research we wanted to evaluate Vale as it is, off-the-shelf, so we did not modify Vale at all.

Verification Times: Perhaps the greatest challenge we face with using Vale is that while the bytecode instructions themselves are often fast to verify, there can be long waits (greater than 10 s) and inconsistent verification results for larger or complicated procedures. Often this process can be assisted with lemmas and assertions, however adding these components is undesirable for developers, and procedures with excessive assertions are difficult to read. The Vale/F* system is supposed to verify each Vale procedure in a modular fashion, but we found that verification times slow down significantly when we work on higher-level procedures that call several lower levels of procedures, and that it is frequently necessary to add low-level lemmas into the Vale code to get verification to succeed. This suggests that the verification is not fully modular, which becomes a significant problem when many levels of procedure calls are used. Vale does offer a 'QuickCode' pre-evaluation process in the host language (F*) to avoid expanding out large verification conditions into Z3 [11], but this has significant overhead in writing which makes evolution of the semantics more difficult, and does not necessarily solve the modularity problem. Vale uses standard Hoare Logic, which provides only coarse modifies clauses for memory updates, so it is possible that adding support for separation logic [21] into Vale could make specifications less verbose and improve verification times, but this would require major changes to Vale.

Printing: The final difficulty we face with Vale is implementing the EVM bytecode printer to convert our verified procedures into executable EVM code. F* must be converted to OCaml to be printed[7] and appears to be very sensitive to the versions and set up. We have been able to run printer examples directly from the F* directory, however we are unable to run the printer examples that come with the latest version of Vale.

6   Related Work

There has been significant research on verification and static analysis of smart contracts written in high-level languages such as Solidity [14], but here we focus on research related to verification of EVM bytecode programs.

Hildenbrant *et al.* present KEVM [15], a tool that offers verification of EVM bytecode programs through the K framework. The K framework offers supporting tools, however relevant to this paper, KEVM has an EVM interpreter and accurate semantics that passes all EVM common tests[8].

Grishchenko *et al.* [13] also have an accurate semantics in their paper, and a partial encoding in F* which could be used for bytecode program verification, however when we attempted to compile and generate OCaml from F* there were issues with outdated F* and OCaml libraries.

Bhargavan *et al.* [4] give a translation of a subset of Solidity into F* and use the F* effect-checking system to catch various error patterns such as re-entrancy

---

[7] F* can also be converted to F# for printing, however the F* documentation claims this is unreliable and encourages using OCaml instead.

[8] https://github.com/ethereum/tests.

and failure to check the result status of external calls. They also translate a subset of EVM bytecode into F*, to check various low-level properties such as bounds on gas consumption. Their uses of F* were focused more on static checking of contract properties, whereas we aim at using F* to verify full functional correctness.

Cassez *et al.* [5] have developed an EVM interpreter in Dafny that offers EVM bytecode verification, furthermore their encoded semantics passes most of the common EVM tests, with the remaining tests failing due to the translation from Dafny into an executable language such as Java to run the tests.

Other tools exist which offer static analysis of EVM bytecode for specific purposes such as: detection of 'out of gas' errors [2,12], ensuring 'effective callback-freedom' to protect from re-entrancy [3], bytecode optimisation to reduce gas [6].

7 Conclusion

We have successfully encoded EVM-R, a subset of EVM, into F*. The F* encoding of EVM-R forms the underlying verification framework for EVM-Vale, a Vale project that raises the EVM-R bytecodes to an intermediate language. EVM-Vale provides the ability to develop EVM bytecode smart contracts, and offers full automatic verification with respect to the EVM-R semantics. Furthermore, EVM-Vale allows refinements to the EVM-R semantics which can be used to verify desired safety properties are maintained in developed smart contracts. We offer refinements to EVM-R bytecodes that maintain safety properties of integer overflow protection, and uninitialised memory access protection. We have demonstrated the ability of Vale to verify non-trival and popular industry relevant smart contracts through our two case studies that are fully verified within our restrictions, and maintain our previously mentioned safety properties.

Specifications written in the Vale language are easy to express and syntactic sugar and custom operators are available, making specifying smart contracts pleasant and likely accessible to most smart contract developers. However the error reporting in terms of the underlying verification framework F* may prove a barrier if developers are unfamiliar with the language.

Overall, Vale offers the ability to verify EVM bytecode, however as a tool it is not yet user friendly or supported well enough to be competitive with other options. A smart contract programmer that desires full verification at the bytecode level would likely be more productive with the already established KEVM, or the promising EVM Dafny. However, if the Vale language was extended to support more flexible expression syntax and to overcome the challenges mentioned above, then it could be a useful platform for verifying EVM bytecode directly as well as lifting reasoning to higher-level procedures for common code patterns.

References

1. Ahrendt, W., et al.: Verification of smart contract business logic. In: Hojjat, H., Massink, M. (eds.) FSEN 2019. LNCS, vol. 11761, pp. 228–243. Springer, Cham (2019). https://doi.org/10.1007/978-3-030-31517-7_16

2. Albert, E., Gordillo, P., Rubio, A., Sergey, I.: Running on fumes. In: Ganty, P., Kaâniche, M. (eds.) VECoS 2019. LNCS, vol. 11847, pp. 63–78. Springer, Cham (2019). https://doi.org/10.1007/978-3-030-35092-5_5

3. Albert, E., Grossman, S., Rinetzky, N., Rodríguez-Núñez, C., Rubio, A., Sagiv, M.: Taming callbacks for smart contract modularity. Proc. ACM Program. Lang. 4(OOPSLA) (2020). https://doi.org/10.1145/3428277

4. Bhargavan, K., et al.: Formal verification of smart contracts: short paper. In: ACM Workshop on Programming Languages and Analysis for Security. Vienna, Austria, October 2016. https://doi.org/10.1145/2993600.2993611, https://inria.hal.science/hal-01400469

5. Cassez, F., Fuller, J., Ghale, M.K., Pearce, D.J., Quiles, H.M.A.: Formal and executable semantics of the ethereum virtual machine in dafny. In: Chechik, M., Katoen, J.P., Leucker, M. (eds.) Formal Methods, pp. 571–583. Springer International Publishing, Cham (2023). https://doi.org/10.1007/978-3-031-27481-7_32

6. Chen, T., et al.: Towards saving money in using smart contracts. In: Proceedings of the 40th International Conference on Software Engineering: New Ideas and Emerging Results, ICSE-NIER 2018, pp. 81–84. Association for Computing Machinery, New York, NY, USA (2018). https://doi.org/10.1145/3183399.3183420

7. Denney, E.: Refinement types for specification. In: Gries, D., de Roever, W.-P. (eds.) Programming Concepts and Methods PROCOMET '98. ITIFIP, pp. 148–166. Springer, Boston, MA (1998). https://doi.org/10.1007/978-0-387-35358-6_13

8. Ethereum: Introduction to smart contracts, August 2022. https://docs.soliditylang.org/en/v0.8.18/introduction-to-smart-contracts.html, Accessed 2 Feb 2023

9. Etherscan: Ethereum unique addresses chart, December 2022, https://etherscan.io/chart/address, Accessed 11 Dec 2022

10. Etherscan: top accounts by eth balance, December 2022, https://etherscan.io/accounts/c, Accessed 11 Dec 2022

11. Fromherz, A., Giannarakis, N., Hawblitzel, C., Parno, B., Rastogi, A., Swamy, N.: A verified, efficient embedding of a verifiable assembly language. In: Principles of Programming Languages (POPL 2019), ACM, January 2019. https://www.microsoft.com/en-us/research/publication/a-verified-efficient-embedding-of-a-verifiable-assembly-language/

12. Grech, N., Kong, M., Jurisevic, A., Brent, L., Scholz, B., Smaragdakis, Y.: Madmax: surviving out-of-gas conditions in ethereum smart contracts. Proc. ACM Program. Lang. 2(OOPSLA) (2018). https://doi.org/10.1145/3276486

13. Grishchenko, I., Maffei, M., Schneidewind, C.: A semantic framework for the security analysis of ethereum smart contracts. In: Bauer, L., Küsters, R. (eds.) POST 2018. LNCS, vol. 10804, pp. 243–269. Springer, Cham (2018). https://doi.org/10.1007/978-3-319-89722-6_10

14. Hajdu, Á., Jovanović, D.: SOLC-VERIFY: a modular verifier for solidity smart contracts. In: Chakraborty, S., Navas, J.A. (eds.) VSTTE 2019. LNCS, vol. 12031, pp. 161–179. Springer, Cham (2020). https://doi.org/10.1007/978-3-030-41600-3_11

15. Hildenbrandt, E., et al.: KEVM: a complete formal semantics of the ethereum virtual machine. In: 31st IEEE Computer Security Foundations Symposium, CSF 2018, Oxford, United Kingdom, 9–12 July 2018, pp. 204–217. IEEE Computer Society (2018). https://doi.org/10.1109/CSF.2018.00022

16. Jiao, J., Kan, S., Lin, S.W., Sanan, D., Liu, Y., Sun, J.: Semantic understanding of smart contracts: executable operational semantics of solidity. In: 2020 IEEE Symposium on Security and Privacy (SP), pp. 1695–1712 (2020). https://doi.org/10.1109/SP40000.2020.00066

17. Marmsoler, D., Brucker, A.D.: A denotational semantics of solidity in Isabelle/HOL. In: Calinescu, R., Păsăreanu, C.S. (eds.) SEFM 2021. LNCS, vol. 13085, pp. 403–422. Springer, Cham (2021). https://doi.org/10.1007/978-3-030-92124-8_23

18. Meyer, B.: Applying 'design by contract'. Computer **25**(10), 40–51 (1992). https://doi.org/10.1109/2.161279

19. Morgan, C.: Programming from Specifications (2nd Ed.). Prentice Hall International (UK) Ltd., GBR (1994)

20. rekt: leaderboard, December 2022. https://rekt.news/leaderboard/, Accessed 11 Dec 2022

21. Reynolds, J.: Separation logic: a logic for shared mutable data structures. In: Proceedings 17th Annual IEEE Symposium on Logic in Computer Science, pp. 55–74 (2002). https://doi.org/10.1109/LICS.2002.1029817

22. Wood, G., et al.: Ethereum: a secure decentralised generalised transaction ledger. Ethereum Project Yellow Paper **151**(2014), 1–32 (2014), Accessed 24 10 2022

23. Zakrzewski, J.: Towards verification of ethereum smart contracts: a formalization of core of solidity. In: Piskac, R., Rümmer, P. (eds.) VSTTE 2018. LNCS, vol. 11294, pp. 229–247. Springer, Cham (2018). https://doi.org/10.1007/978-3-030-03592-1_13

Detecting Malicious Blockchain Transactions Using Graph Neural Networks

Samantha Tharani Jeyakumar[1](✉) [iD],
Andrew Charles Eugene Yugarajah[2](✉) [iD], Zhé Hóu[1](✉) [iD],
and Vallipuram Muthukkumarasamy[1](✉) [iD]

[1] Griffith University, Brisbane, Australia
jeyakumar.samanthatharani@griffithuni.edu.au,
{z.hou,v.muthu}@griffith.edu.au
[2] University of Jaffna, Jaffna, Sri Lanka
charles.ey@univ.jfn.ac.lk

Abstract. The adoption of blockchain technology within various critical infrastructures is on the rise. Concurrently, there has been a corresponding increase in its misuse, primarily through the exploitation of its pseudo-anonymous characteristic. Encouraging blockchain adoption and improving security in the decentralised environment require techniques to detect wallets and/or smart contracts owned by malicious entities. Illegal activities such as dark market trades, money laundering, and receiving unlawful payments are performed by connecting various wallets or smart contracts in a meticulous way. A graph can be a potential representation to visualise such interconnections via various patterns, and graph-based data may represent the topological structure of the blockchain network. Recently, Graph Neural Networks (GNN) have been widely used for analysing the structure of complex networks and identifying patterns. This is the first work that considers a generalised graph representation for the Bitcoin and Ethereum networks and analyses their behaviour using a combination of heterogeneous GNN framework's GraphSAGE and Graph Attention Network (GAT). The classification results reveal that the proposed approach modestly improved Bitcoin network analysis, whereas Ethereum smart contract analysis needs further investigation in terms of incorporating other aspects of smart contracts, such as codebase, byte length, and lifetime features.

Keywords: blockchain · ransomewre settlement · ponzi smart contract · graph-based analysis

1 Introduction

Blockchain is a distributed and decentralised digital ledger technology that records transactions securely and transparently. Key properties of this technology include immutability, transparency, pseudo-anonymity, and decentralisation, making it suitable for various applications: tracking manufacturing in

N. Dong et al. (Eds.): SDLT 2023, CCIS 1975, pp. 55–71, 2024.
https://doi.org/10.1007/978-981-97-0006-6_4

the supply chain, health record and insurance claim monitoring, peer-to-peer energy trading, and secure data sharing in IoT [4,9]. The pseudo-anonymity ensures the privacy of participants in blockchain networks. Malicious actors that are receiving ransomware or phishing payments in the form of cryptocurrency, involving dark-market trades, and dealing with money laundering exploited the pseudo-anonymous property to obscure their real identity from legal authorities or financial regulators. For instance, approximately $3.36 billion worth of dark web-related transactions concealed within Silk Road were Seized and those responsible were convicted in 2021, as reported by the U.S. Attorney. Such misuse holds the potential to gradually diminish public confidence in the widespread acceptance of blockchain technology. Additionally, these illegal activities present regulatory challenges in ensuring that the technology is not manipulated for malicious intentions. Preventing illegal activities and supporting the implementation of regularity schemes are urgently needed in the monitoring and analysis of blockchain networks. Large volumes and complex structures of blockchain transactions are significant limitations for the analysis. An efficient analysis needs a meaningful transformation for blockchain data that can inform the interconnection between wallets, smart contracts, and their transactions. A graph is a well-defined data structure for representing relations between different types of nodes and can reflect the interconnections via graph patterns [6,7,16,26].

Graph-based analysis can fall into three categories: node classification, edge classification, and graph classification. The graph-based analysis for blockchain transactions can be beneficial in terms of node classification to classify the behaviour of wallets, smart contracts, or transactions or graph classification to identify groups of wallets owned by mixing services or dark markets. Literature study has identified previous research work using graph-based representation and analysis to identify mixing services [24,27,31], dark market-related trades [20], and Ponzi schemes [32] in Bitcoin and Ethereum networks. The existing studies involved manual processes, domain knowledge, focused on a specific blockchain network, and inefficient resource utilisation. Heuristics-based analysis is mostly subjective based on the selected domain or attack. By considering these limitations and challenges this study made the following contributions.

1. The proposed study considered a generalised graph modelling known as a hypergraph, which allows the analysis of blockchain networks without concern for the different structures of transaction data.
2. Embedding feature generation for this study considered both raw and interconnection information of address-to-transaction and smart contract-to-transaction. This is useful to train a model by considering the self and relational features of nodes (wallet and smart contracts).
3. This is the first study performed on graph-based learning using heterogenous GNN frameworks by combining GraphSAGE and GAT GNNs. The result leads to the implementation of a heterogenous GNN model for real-time blockchain network analysis to identify suspicious behaviour of wallet or smart contracts.

The structure of the paper is as follows: Sect. 2 presents a critical review of related studies of GNN-based blockchain network analysis. Section 3 describes the proposed heterogenous GNN-based classification. Section 4 presents classification results for blockchain transactions and discusses the significance of the proposed GNN-based analysis. Finally, Sect. 5 concludes the paper.

2 Related Work

This section details existing research works related to suspicious transaction detection in blockchain networks. The recent research approaches used Artificial Neural Networks (ANN) [20], Deep autoencoder [24], Convolution Neural Network [22], Graph Convolution Networks (GCN) [30,32], and Random Forest [12,21] to classify malicious blockchain transactions.

Lee et al. [20] proposed a supervised learning approach using Random Forest (RF) and Artificial Neural Networks (ANN) to classify malicious Bitcoin transactions related to Silk Road dark market trades. Their ANN-based network is designed with an input layer, two hidden layers, and an output layer. Transaction features considered for the classification reflect the number of inputs, outputs, and their values. Noticeably, their classification does not consider the interconnection information between wallet and transactions.

Lihao Nan et al. [24] proposed an address graph-embedding feature-based approach to identify the community of mixing services on the Bitcoin network. They obtained graph embedding features using a deep auto-encoder and fed them into a k-means clustering to identify the community clusters. The local outlier probabilities [19] used in their approach identified nodes related to mixing services. The identified limitations in their approach are the local outlier probabilities method is much slower for large-scale graphs, there are no address-based features involved in the node embedding, and the experiment was not tested with real mixing data.

Mark Weber et al. [30] used GCN to classify binary class Bitcoin transaction network. Their experiment considered raw transaction features as well as transaction-to-transaction graph data for licit and illicit node classification. Their proposed GCN considered a two-layer, runs 1000 epochs employs the Adam optimizer with a learning rate of 0.001 and utilises an embedding vector size of 100. Considerably, their proposed approach is only applicable to the Bitcoin network.

Shanquing Yu et al. [32] proposed a graph convolutional network-based classification model to identify Ponzi scheme smart contracts using transaction networks. They obtained fourteen raw features of smart contracts and node-embedding features of transaction networks. A 32-dimension node embedding vector was obtained using a three-layer GCN architecture. Their classification considered supervised learning approaches: linear regression [23], support vector machine [13], adaptive learning rate optimisation [17], and random forest [8], network embedding-based approach: LINE [28], random-walk-based approaches: deepwalk [25] and node2vec [10]. They found that the combination of basic features with the GCN outperforms the other methods.

Lou et al. [22] proposed an improved convolution neural network to analyse the bytecode image of smart contracts to predict Ponzi schemes. Their proposed approach outperformed the supervised learning approaches Random Forest, support vector machine, XGBoost, and Isolation forest. Noticeably, their proposed preprocessing for bytecodes of each smart contract slows down when a large amount of training and testing data is used.

Xuezhi He et al. [12] proposed a decision tree-based supervised learning approach called Code and Transaction Random Forest (CTRF) to identify Ponzi contracts on Ethereum networks. Their experimental dataset considered word and sequence features of smart contract's code, and transaction features. The dataset was validated against supervised learning approaches KNN, CNN, decision tree, SVM, XGBoost, and CTRF. Their experimental results identified that the sequence feature of smart contract opcode and the transaction features improved model performance in identifying Ponzi contracts.

Lo et al. [21] proposed a GNN framework based on self-supervised Deep Graph Infomax (DGI) and Graph Isomorphism Network (GIN), with Random Forest (RF). Their proposed approach first constructs embedding vectors for Bitcoin transaction networks and then uses them as features to train RF to classify money laundering transactions. Results revealed that their proposed approach outperforms the traditional approaches and obtained a 0.828 F1-score.

The existing approaches stated above involved manual processes, domain knowledge, and high resource utilisation. Heuristics-based node labelling is primarily subjective based on the selected domain or attack. Considering these limitations and challenges, this research work provides an automated generalised graph modelling and GNN-based analysis framework to classify various anomalous behaviours of nodes in blockchain networks.

3   Methodology

This section details the proposed approach for Graph Neural Networks (GNNs) based analysis to classify malicious participants (wallet or transaction or smart contracts). The proposed approach includes four phases: data collection, data modelling, data pre-processing, and analysis, as described in Fig. 1. First, the data collection phase details the experimental data used for generalised graph modelling. Then data modelling phase explains feature extraction [14] of wallet, transactions, smart contracts and graph structure information via hypergraph [15]. Finally, the analysis details the GNN-based classification approaches and their outcomes.

3.1   Data Collection

Data collection describes the scrapping of blockchain transactions for normal and malicious activities in Bitcoin and Ethereum networks. The analysis of this research involves normal & ransomware settlement-based and non-Ponzi & Ponzi scheme-based transactions.

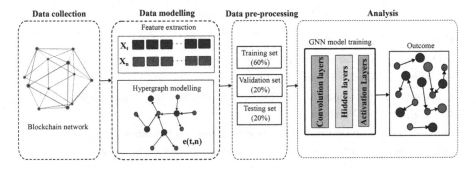

Fig. 1. Overview of the proposed methodology.

Bitcoin Ransomware Transactions. The labels of normal and ransomware settlement-based Bitcoin network wallets were referred from the BitcoinHeist [5] dataset, then recent 100 transactions corresponding with 16938 wallets were captured using public API [1].

Ethereum Ponzi Smart Contract Transactions. The labels of non-Ponzi and Ponzi smart contracts were referred from the public dataset [2] and the detailed information of smart contract transactions was obtained using public API [3]. The collected transactions include 200 Ponzi and 3590 non-Ponzi smart contracts.

3.2 Data Modelling

This section describes node features that are used as inputs for GNN-based analysis. The node features are derived based on raw transaction information and their maximum, minimum, mean, mode, median, and standard deviation measures. Tables 1, 2, and 3 detail major features of Bitcoin transactions, and wallets, and Ethereum smart contract transactions which are used as initial node properties during generation of graph embedding.

Bitcoin Transactions. The graphs of the Bitcoin network considered in this study included two types of nodes: transaction and wallet. A transaction contains nineteen features explained in Table 1, whereas a wallet consists of sixteen features shown in Table 2.

Ethereum Smart Contract Transactions. The graph of the Ethereum network considered in this study involves two types of nodes: transactions and smart contracts. A smart contract transaction contains five features detailed in Table 3, whereas a smart contract address involves sixteen features described in Table 2.

This research aims to propose a generalised approach to analyse any type of blockchain network. Hypergraph G_h is a generalised graph modelling for different types of blockchain transactions which represents the interactions between

Table 1. Features for Bitcoin transaction.

Features	Description
$inDegree$	number of incoming transactions (UTXOs)
$outDegree$	number of outgoing transactions
$totalInput$	total amount of Bitcoins received from other transactions (UTXO)
$totalOutput$	total amount of Bitcoin sent
$inout - ratio$	ratio between the number of inputs and outputs
$unique - out$	number of unique output addresses involved in a transaction

Table 2. Features for Bitcoin wallets and smart contract addresses.

Features	Description
$asASender$	total number of times a specific address as a sender
$asAReceiver$	total number of times a specific address as a receiver
$totalSpent$	total amount spent by a specific address
$totalReceive$	total amount received by a specific address

Table 3. Node features for Ethereum transactions.

Feature	Description
$betweeness_t$	betweenness centrality value between the transaction and the smart contract
$closness_t$	closeness centrality value between the transaction and the smart contract
$degree_t$	degree centrality value between the transaction and the smart contract
$eigenvector_t$	eigenvector centrality value between the transaction and the smart contract
$balance_t$	balance after the transaction

transactions and wallets or smart contracts. Edge information $e(u, v)$ indicates the type of transaction v (spent or received) corresponding with the wallet or smart contracts u. For this reason, we select a hypergraph that is proposed in the research [15] to extract the graph structure features. Further, these features facilitate training a single model to analyse various types of nodes in the blockchain network. This study considers Bitcoin transactions related to normal and ransomware settlements and Ethereum transactions related to non-Ponzi and Ponzi smart contracts. In the Bitcoin hypergraph, nodes are wallets (normal and ransomware-related) and their transactions. Edges are the type of transaction (spent or received) corresponding with wallets. Bitcoin transactions contain two major elements namely inputs and outputs. Inputs detail the Unspent Transaction Outputs (UTXOs), and outputs explain where the UTXOs are spent. In ransomware settlements inputs represent bitcoins received from the victims and the outputs indicate the wallet that accumulated all bitcoins from the victims. Figure 2 depicts an example of hypergraphs obtained for ransomware settlements, using the experimental data detailed in Sect. 3.1.

In the Ethereum hypergraph, nodes are smart contracts (non-Ponzi and Ponzi) and their transactions. Edges are the type of transaction (spent or received) corresponding with smart contracts. The main elements of Ethereum smart contract transactions are the address of the smart contract, details of the transaction that invoked the smart contract or invoked by the smart contract, and the amount spent/received during contract invocation. In Ponzi scheme settlements, ether was received from new investors and spent immediately for earlier investors. Figure 3 depicts an example of hypergraphs obtained for Ponzi smart contract settlements from the experimental data described in Sect. 3.1.

3.3   Data Pre-processing

The data pre-processing phase received node properties and graph structure-based data from the data modelling phase and divided them into training, validation, and testing sets. This study considered 60% of data for training, 20% of data for validation and 20% of data for testing. Table 4 presents the amount of data considered in each of the three sets of Bitcoin and Ethereum networks.

Table 4. Data allocation for classification.

Blockchain	Node type	Training	Validation	Testing
Bitcoin	Transactions	17122	6423	6354
	Addresses	10162	3388	3388
	Edge list	21896	7593	7213
Ethereum smart contract	Transactions	4707	1740	1766
	Addresses	240	80	80
	Edge list	4707	1740	1766

3.4   Grap Neural Network-Based (GNN) Analysis

This section details Grap Neural Network (GNN)-based analysis to classify malicious wallets or smart contracts and their transactions in blockchain networks as shown in Fig. 1. The proposed GNN-based approach contains three layers: the input layer, the GNN layer, and the prediction layer. A detailed description of each layer is as follows:

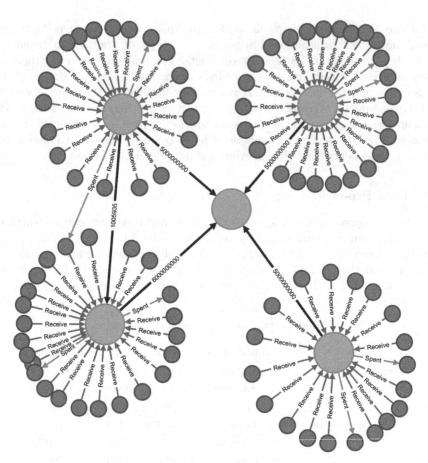

Fig. 2. Hypergraph for ransomware settlement. Here blue circles are transactions, orange circles are the wallets, red arrows represent inputs and green ones are the outputs. (Color figure online)

Input Layer: The input layer consists of node features, edge relations (spent or receive), and graph structure. The features $\alpha_t \in \mathbb{R}$ and $\alpha_n \in \mathbb{R}$ represent transaction features and wallet or smart contract features, respectively. These features are passed as an embedding to d-dimensional hidden features $h_i^{l=0}$ via simple linear projection. The edge information $\beta_{tn} \in \mathbb{R}$ consider the type of transactions (received or spent) corresponding with a wallet or smart contract. Similar to the node features, edge information is also considered for embedding to d-dimensional hidden feature $e_{ij}^{l=0}$. Finally, graph structure $e(t, n)$, from hypergraphs inputs as connection information where t is a spending or receiving transaction and n can be a wallet or smart contract.

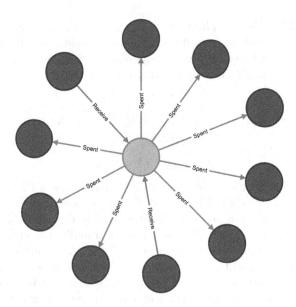

Fig. 3. Hypergraph for Ponzi smart contract. Here yellow circle represents the Ponzi smart contract, the blue circles represent the transactions, the red arrows spending transactions, and the green ones represent receiving transactions. (Color figure online)

$L\times$ **GNN Layer:** The GNN layer consists of the L layer neural network. The L layer deep network corresponds to $L-$hop neighbourhood aggregation across the entire network. This is an iterative process, which can be visualised as a message-passing mechanism where each node (wallet/smart contract/transaction) receives updates from all its neighbours. The updated feature vector h_i^{l+1} for wallet or smart contract or transaction i is simply a function of its previous feature vector h_i^l and feature vectors of all its neighbours j as described in Eq. (1).

$$h_i^{l+1} = f(h_i^{l+1}, h_j^l : j \rightarrow i) \tag{1}$$

The blockchain network involves different types of nodes, changes dynamically, and is large in volume. By considering these constraints, this study used two heterogeneous GNN models Graph Attention Network Convolution (GAT) [29] and the GraphSAGE Convolution (SAGE) [11] are the extended versions of Graph Convolution Network (GCN) [18]. The selected convolution networks are capable of considering different types of nodes and their properties during the training. The architecture of GAT needs whole graph information for node representation (embedding), whereas SAGE generates node representation by sampling. Both SAGE and GAT can predict unseen nodes without re-training.

The proposed GNN-based approach for blockchain network analysis utilised both SAGE and GAT convolution layers. Learning details of SAGE and GAT are as follows:

- **GraphSAGE:** The GraphSAGE learns representations for each node by considering information from its neighbouring nodes. GraphSAGE achieved this learning in a two-step process: sampling and aggregation. The detailed description for GraphSAGE embedding is as follows:

$$h_v^0 \leftarrow x_v, \forall v \in V \tag{2}$$

$$h_N(v)^k \leftarrow f_{aggregate}(\{h_u^{k-1} | \ \forall u \in N(v)\}) \tag{3}$$

$$h_v^k \leftarrow \sigma(W^k(h_v^{k-1} \ || \ h_{N(v)}^k)) \tag{4}$$

$$h_v^k \leftarrow h_v^k / ||h_v^k||_2, \forall v \in V \tag{5}$$

At first, all wallets or smart contracts and transactions in the hypergraph are initialised to their original feature vector x_v as described in Eq. (2). Then the feature aggregation at level k is processed as described in Eq. (3), here $N(v)$ denotes a list of neighbours of node v. Finally, the embedding vector at kth level updating via concatenates h_v^{k-1} and $h_{N(v)}^k$ embeddings of wallet or smart contract and transaction, where —— denotes concatenation, then takes a dot product of it and a learnable weight vector $\vec{W}^k$ and applies an activation function σ in the end as stated in Eq. (4). The general distribution of node embedding is achieved in GraphSAGE via normalisation as in Eq. (5).

- **GAT:** Graph Attention Network Convolution (GAT) employs attention mechanisms to determine how much focus each node in a graph should give to its neighbouring nodes. The attention mechanism allows nodes to selectively aggregate information from their neighbours, giving more weight to nodes that are more relevant to the current task. The details of the attention mechanism are as follows:

$$z_i^{(l)} = W^{(l)} h_i^{(l)}, \tag{6}$$

$$e_{ij}^{(l)} = LeakyReLU(\vec{U}^{(l)T}(z_i^{(l)} || z_j^{(l)})), \tag{7}$$

$$\alpha_{ij}^{(l)} = \frac{exp(e_{ij}^{(l)})}{\sum_{k \in N(i)} exp(e_{ik}^{(l)})}, \tag{8}$$

$$h_i^{(l+1)} = \sigma(\sum_{j \in N(i)} \alpha_{ij}^{(l)} z_j^{(l)}) \tag{9}$$

The linear transformation of lower layer embedding $h_i^{(l)}$ of a wallet or smart contract and transaction and their learnable weight matrix $W^{(l)}$ approached as described in Eq. (6). A pair-wise un-normalised attention score between a wallet or smart contract and its neighbour transactions computes via concatenates z embeddings of the wallet or smart contract and the transaction then takes a dot product of it and a learnable weight vector $\vec{U}^{(l)}$ and applies a *LeakyReLU* in the end as detailed in Eq. (7). A softmax operation applies to normalise the attention scores on each node's incoming edges as detailed in Eq. (8). Finally, the embeddings from the neighbours are aggregated together and scaled by the attention scores as in Eq. (9).

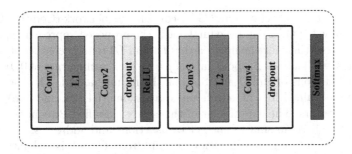

Fig. 4. Structure of the proposed GNN network for the analysis of blockchain network. Here, *Conv*1, *Conv*2, *Conv*3, and *Conv*4 represent the SAGE or/and GAT convolution layers, $L1$, and $L2$ are the liner layers, and dropout value $p = 0.2$. *ReLU* and *Softmax* are the activation functions.

The proposed GNN-based approach shown in Fig. 4 choose $L = 4$ and align Conv1 = GAT, Conv2 = SAGE, Conv3 = GAT, Conv4 = SAGE, liner layers $L1$ and $L2$, dropout value $p = 0.2$, learning rate 0.01, and the activation functions *ReLU* and *Softmax*. The alignment of the SAGE convolution layer followed by the GAT convolution layer, first extracts the aggregate information from the target wallet's or smart contract's neighbour transactions, giving more weight to transactions that are more relevant to normal or malicious settlement behaviour. This weighted outcome provides an informative sample for the SAGE layer and improves the learning of the classification models.

Prediction Layer: The prediction layer utilises GNN-based node embedding outcomes to predict malicious wallets or smart contracts and transactions in Bitcoin and Ethereum networks. In this layer, we designed a cross entropy-based loss function, Adam optimiser for model optimisation, and applied gradient descent to improve classification. This helps the proposed GNN-based approach learn more task-based discriminative node embeddings for each wallet, smart contracts and transactions.

4   Evaluation

This section first details the experimental setup and the classification results obtained for hypergraph-based Graph Neural Network (GNN) analysis. Further, this section analyses and discusses the significance of the proposed approach by comparing the results reported in related works. The implementation of the proposed graph-based analysis was carried out on a computer with Ubuntu 22.04.2 LTS x86_64, 12th Gen Intel i9-12900 and 16085MiB/ 128511MiB, and PyTorch geometric with 3.10 kernel version.

The experimental setup of this study considered three different experimental setups using combinations of selected convolution networks. The first setup only considered the SAGE convolution network (Conv1 = Conv2 = Conv3 = Conv 4

= SAGE). Second, only considered GAT convolution network (Conv1 = Conv2 = Conv3 = Conv 4 = GAT) and the final one is the proposed approach explained in Sect. 3.4. The settings for the linear layers $L1$ and $L2$ remain consistent across all three setups, with a fixed dropout rate of $p = 0.2$, a learning rate of 0.01, and the activation functions of ReLU and Softmax being unchanged. The classification results were obtained for three different dimensions (64,128, and 256) of graph embedding vectors. The experiment of this study classified Bitcoin transactions and wallets, Ethereum smart contract transactions and addresses.

During the training, d dimension output from $Conv1$ is fed into a linear layer to obtain d dimensional linear output. The liner outputs are then fed into $Conv2$, which provides another d dimensional embedding vector. The output vectors produced by $Conv2$ are passed to the dropout layer with $p = 0.2$ to prevent overfitting during training. The output of the dropout layer is passed through a $ReLU$ activation function to ensure that negative neuron outputs are rectified to zero. The outcome of the $ReLU$ is transferred to $Conv3$ and produces a two-dimensional vector of values. The outcome is passed to the linear layer $L2$ to obtain linear output values. Then the linearly transformed outcomes are fed to the $Conv4$ layer and provide another two-dimensional vector of values. The outcome from the $Con4$ layer is fed to the dropout layer with $p = 0.2$ to prevent overfitting during training. Finally, the $Softmax$ layer processes the outcomes to ensure that the output values are between 0 and 1, representing the probability of each class (normal or malicious) for each type of node (wallet/smart contract/transaction). The output from the $Softmax$ is compared with the actual labels of wallet or smart contracts or transactions to identify loss. The loss value is fed back to the Adam optimiser to update the weights in each hidden layer for a new round of training. These iterations (500 epochs) increase the classification accuracy for the training set. Finally, a test set is used to obtain precision, recall, and F1 scores. These evaluation measures were selected to compare the experimental results with the results presented in literature studies.

Table 5 presents results for the classification of normal and malicious Bitcoin transactions. The 64 and 256 dimensions of the proposed GNN-based approach achieved high precision, recall, and F1-score, whereas for 128 dimensions SAGE convolution obtained the highest result. Based on the classification result for Ethereum smart contract transactions presented in Table 6 the proposed approach obtained a high precision, recall, and F1-score for 64 and 128 dimensions, whereas SAGE convolution obtained a high recall and F1-score for 256 dimensions.

The classification results for Bitcoin wallets are presented in Table 7 specifies that for 64 and 128 dimensions, the proposed approach obtained high precision, recall, and F1-score, whereas for 256 dimensions GraphSAGE obtained the best results. Results for the Ethereum smart contract address classification are detailed in Table 8, which reveals that for all dimensions of embedding vectors the proposed approach obtained a high recall and F1-score. For 128 and 256 dimensions, the GAT obtained the highest precision value.

Overall, the proposed GNN obtained a 0.8978 F1-score for Bitcoin transactions with 256 dimensions and a 0.8857 F1-score for Bitcoin wallets with 128 dimensions. For the Ethereum smart contracts, the proposed GNN obtained a 0.8481 F1-score with 256 dimensions for transactions and a 0.8399 F1-score with 64 dimensions for addresses. The learning time of the proposed GNN is comparatively higher than the SAGE-based GNN and less than the GAT-based GNN.

Table 5. Classification results for Bitcoin transactions.

GNN	Dimension of the embedding vector								
	d = 64			d = 128			d = 256		
	Precision	Recall	F1	Precision	Recall	F1	Precision	Recall	F1
SAGE	0.8796	0.8169	0.8471	0.9140	0.8716	**0.8923**	0.8061	0.7404	0.7719
GAT	0.8344	0.8534	0.8438	0.8842	0.8095	0.8452	0.8863	0.8265	0.8554
Proposed GNN	0.8988	0.8828	**0.8907**	0.9104	0.8538	0.8812	0.9223	0.8745	**0.8978**

Table 6. Classification results for smart contract transactions.

GNN	Dimension of the embedding vector								
	d = 64			d = 128			d = 256		
	Precision	Recall	F1	Precision	Recall	F1	Precision	Recall	F1
SAGE	0.6908	0.9501	0.8000	0.6815	0.9239	0.7844	0.6912	0.9534	0.8013
GAT	0.8667	0.6116	0.7172	0.8882	0.6558	0.7545	0.8501	0.8021	0.8254
Proposed GNN	0.8499	0.8430	**0.8464**	0.9615	0.6950	**0.8068**	0.9050	0.8414	**0.8720**

The classification results presented in Table 5 to 8 reveal the significance of the hypergraph-based GNN classification and the proposed GNN-based approach via high evaluation scores.

The comparison for binary class classification results of the Bitcoin transactions is provided in Table 5 and results presented in related studies are detailed in Table 9. There is no related literature for Bitcoin wallet classification, hence

Table 7. Classification results for Bitcoin wallets.

GNN	Dimension of the embedding vector								
	d = 64			d = 128			d = 256		
	Precision	Recall	F1	Precision	Recall	F1	Precision	Recall	F1
SAGE	0.8436	0.8926	0.8674	0.8508	0.8680	0.8594	0.8212	0.9094	**0.8631**
GAT	0.8410	0.8758	0.8581	0.8176	0.8221	0.8199	0.7956	0.8535	0.8235
Proposed GNN	0.8576	0.9027	**0.8796**	0.8746	0.8971	**0.8857**	0.8385	0.8826	0.8599

Table 8. Classification results for smart contract addresses.

GNN	Dimension of the embedding vector								
	d = 64			d = 128			d = 256		
	Precision	Recall	F1	Precision	Recall	F1	Precision	Recall	F1
SAGE	0.5846	0.8085	0.6786	0.5735	0.6783	0.8297	0.5946	0.9362	0.7273
GAT	0.7742	0.5106	0.6154	0.8387	0.5532	0.6667	0.7813	0.6329	0.5319
Proposed GNN	0.7924	0.8936	**0.8399**	0.7679	0.9149	**0.8349**	0.7288	0.9149	**0.8113**

no comparison details are provided. Similarly, the comparison of classification results of Ethereum smart contract addresses are provided in Table 8 and the results reported in the literature are detailed in Table 9.

Table 9. Comparison details for the classification results obtained via proposed GNN and the results in the related literature.

Blockchain	Approach	F1-score
Bitcoin	Artificial Neural Network	0.8854 [20]
	Deep Autoencoder	0.2081 [24]
	Graph Convolution Network	0.628 [30]
	Inspection-L	0.828 [21]
	Proposed GNN	**0.8978**
Ethereum	GCN	0.8963 [32]
	CNN	**0.959** [22]
	Code and Transaction Random Forest (CTRF)	0.909 [12]
	Proposed GNN	0.8399

Based on Table 9 the proposed GNN-based approach produced the most promising results for Bitcoin networks. Whereas, the results for the Ethereum smart contracts reveal the significance of the smart contract features related to code structure, byte contract length, and lifetime in the identification of suspicious behaviour [12] and [22].

The unique graph patterns for ransomware settlements and Ponzi contracts shown in Fig. 2 and Fig. 3 reveal that to distinguish the behaviour of the normal and malicious Bitcoin wallets we have to focus on up to four hops, whereas for the smart contract, it's only one. This could be the reason for the decrease in classification performance when $L > 4$. In terms of the dimension of the vector, the performance gets reduced when $d < 64$ or $d > 256$.

The main limitation of the above analysis is that the study was performed using transaction data stored in a local machine. The transaction node's properties used for smart contract analysis do not consider the raw data and code-based features.

Future work will investigate an improved GNN-based approach for Ethereum network analysis and integrate the proposed approach for a real-time and interactive monitoring tool to enhance the decision-making of end-users at blockchain-based systems, including critical infrastructures, by providing meaningful visualisation and early warnings.

5   Conclusion

This research work investigated the effectiveness of generalised heterogeneous graph modelling and proposed a GNN-based approach to predict malicious wallets and/ or smart contracts and their transactions in blockchain networks. The proposed hypergraph-based GNN analysis gave promising F1 scores for the prediction of malicious wallets, smart contracts, and transactions. The results obtained for Bitcoin network classification based on the proposed approach achieved marginal improvement compared to the results reported in related studies. The Ethereum smart contract-based classification results indicate the need for including the code and lifetime-based features of smart contracts in suspicious behaviour identification. The proposed generalised GNN-based approach may integrate with the real-time blockchain network to monitor and analyse malicious behaviour. Such integration is beneficial in terms of prompt alerts or early warnings for forensic analysers, law enforcement authorities, and financial regulators to maintain a secure and trusted blockchain ecosystem, which is essential for the adoption and success of blockchain technology across various industries.

References

1. Blockchain data API (2021). https://www.blockchain.com/api/blockchain_api
2. Ponzi smart contract (2021). https://www.kaggle.com/datasets/xblock/smart-ponzi-scheme-labels
3. Ethereum transaction dataset (2022). https://api.blockcypher.com/v1/eth/main/txs/
4. Jeyakumar, S.T., Ko, R., Muthukkumarasamy, V.: A framework for user-centric visualisation of blockchain transactions in critical infrastructure. In: Proceedings of the 5th ACM International Symposium on Blockchain and Secure Critical Infrastructure (BSCI 2023), pp. 44–52. Association for Computing Machinery, New York, USA (2023). https://doi.org/10.1145/3594556.3594624
5. Akcora, C.G., Li, Y., Gel, Y.R., Kantarcioglu, M.: Bitcoinheist: topological data analysis for ransomware detection on the bitcoin blockchain. arXiv preprint [Web Link] (2019)
6. Akoglu, L., Tong, H., Koutra, D.: Graph-based anomaly detection and description: a survey (2014)
7. Brambilla, M., Javadian Sabet, A., Kharmale, K., Sulistiawati, A.E.: Graph-based conversation analysis in social media. Big Data Cogn. Comput. 6(4) (2022). https://doi.org/10.3390/bdcc6040113, https://www.mdpi.com/2504-2289/6/4/113

8. Breiman, L.: Random forests. Mach. Learn. **45**, 5–32 (2001)
9. Di Francesco Maesa, D., Mori, P.: Blockchain 3.0 applications survey (2020)
10. Grover, A., Leskovec, J.: node2vec: Scalable feature learning for networks. In: Proceedings of the 22nd ACM SIGKDD International Conference on Knowledge Discovery and Data Mining, pp. 855–864 (2016)
11. Hamilton, W.L., Ying, R., Leskovec, J.: Inductive representation learning on large graphs (2018)
12. He, X., Yang, T., Chen, L.: CTRF: ethereum-based ponzi contract identification. Secur. Commun. Netw. **2022** (2022)
13. Hearst, M.A., Dumais, S.T., Osuna, E., Platt, J., Scholkopf, B.: Support vector machines. IEEE Intell. Syst. Appl. **13**(4), 18–28 (1998)
14. Jeyakumar, S., Eugene Yugarajah, A.C., Rathore, P., Palaniswami, M., Muthukkumarasamy, V., Hóu, Z.: Feature engineering for anomaly detection and classification of blockchain transactions, March 2023. https://doi.org/10.36227/techrxiv.22329805.v1, https://www.techrxiv.org/articles/preprint/Feature_Engineering_for_Anomaly_Detection_and_Classification_of_Blockchain_Transactions/22329805
15. Jeyakumar, S., Hóu, Z., Eugene Yugarajah, A.C., Palaniswami, M., Muthukkumarasamy, V.: Visualizing blockchain transaction behavioural pattern: a graph-based approach, March 2023. https://doi.org/10.36227/techrxiv.22329889.v1, https://www.techrxiv.org/articles/preprint/Visualizing_Blockchain_Transaction_Behavioural_Pattern_A_Graph-based_Approach/22329889
16. Kılıç, B., Özturan, C., Sen, A.: Analyzing large-scale blockchain transaction graphs for fraudulent activities. Big Data Artif. Intell. Digit. Finan. **253** (2022)
17. Kingma, D.P., Ba, J.: Adam: a method for stochastic optimization (2017)
18. Kipf, T.N., Welling, M.: Semi-supervised classification with graph convolutional networks (2017)
19. Kriegel, H.P., Kröger, P., Schubert, E., Zimek, A.: Loop: local outlier probabilities. In: Proceedings of the 18th ACM Conference on Information and Knowledge Management, pp. 1649–1652 (2009)
20. Lee, C., Maharjan, S., Ko, K., Hong, J.W.-K.: Toward detecting illegal transactions on bitcoin using machine-learning methods. In: Zheng, Z., Dai, H.-N., Tang, M., Chen, X. (eds.) BlockSys 2019. CCIS, vol. 1156, pp. 520–533. Springer, Singapore (2020). https://doi.org/10.1007/978-981-15-2777-7_42
21. Lo, W.W., Kulatilleke, G.K., Sarhan, M., Layeghy, S., Portmann, M.: Inspection-l: self-supervised GNN node embeddings for money laundering detection in bitcoin. Appl. Intell. **53**, 1–12 (2023). https://doi.org/10.1007/s10489-023-04504-9
22. Lou, Y., Zhang, Y., Chen, S.: Ponzi contracts detection based on improved convolutional neural network. In: 2020 IEEE International Conference on Services Computing (SCC), pp. 353–360 (2020). https://doi.org/10.1109/SCC49832.2020.00053
23. Montgomery, D.C., Peck, E.A., Vining, G.G.: Introduction to Linear Regression Analysis. Wiley, Hoboken (2021)
24. Nan, L., Tao, D.: Bitcoin mixing detection using deep autoencoder. In: 2018 IEEE Third International Conference on Data Science in Cyberspace (DSC), pp. 280–287. IEEE (2018)
25. Perozzi, B., Al-Rfou, R., Skiena, S.: Deepwalk: online learning of social representations. In: Proceedings of the 20th ACM SIGKDD International Conference on Knowledge Discovery and Data Mining, pp. 701–710 (2014)
26. Samantha Tharani, J., R.K., Muthukkumarasamy, V.: A framework for user-centric visualisation of blockchain transactions in critical infrastructure (2023)

27. Shojaeenasab, A., Motamed, A.P., Bahrak, B.: Mixing detection on bitcoin transactions using statistical patterns. arXiv preprint arXiv:2204.02019 (2022)
28. Tang, J., Qu, M., Wang, M., Zhang, M., Yan, J., Mei, Q.: Line: large-scale information network embedding. In: Proceedings of the 24th International Conference on World Wide Web, pp. 1067–1077 (2015)
29. Veličković, P., Cucurull, G., Casanova, A., Romero, A., Liò, P., Bengio, Y.: Graph attention networks (2018)
30. Weber, M., et al.: Anti-money laundering in bitcoin: experimenting with graph convolutional networks for financial forensics. arXiv preprint arXiv:1908.02591 (2019)
31. Wu, J., Liu, J., Chen, W., Huang, H., Zheng, Z., Zhang, Y.: Detecting mixing services via mining bitcoin transaction network with hybrid motifs. IEEE Trans. Syst. Man Cybern. Syst. **52**(4), 2237–2249 (2021)
32. Yu, S., Jin, J., Xie, Y., Shen, J., Xuan, Q.: Ponzi scheme detection in ethereum transaction network. In: Dai, H.-N., Liu, X., Luo, D.X., Xiao, J., Chen, X. (eds.) BlockSys 2021. CCIS, vol. 1490, pp. 175–186. Springer, Singapore (2021). https://doi.org/10.1007/978-981-16-7993-3_14

Data Sharing Using Verifiable Credentials in the Agriculture Sector

Paul Ashley[⊠]

Anonyome Labs, Gold Coast 4217, Australia
pashley@anonyome.com

Abstract. The agricultural sector faces new challenges. Consumers now expect that food they eat is good for them and good for the environment. Fear of climate change is driving more regulation and data compliance requirements. There are new global standards of data verification requiring agriculture to confirm to these standards for international export. This paper describes the technical implementation details of a Decentralized Agricultural Ecosystem aiming to share data in a secure way; an approach that will allow farmers and growers to capture, manage and share their data while also controlling and protecting it.

Keywords: Verifiable Credentials · Verifiable Data · Decentralized Identity

1 Introduction

Around the world expectations, requirements and standards in the agriculture industry are changing. Greater proof of provenance and or other environmental and marketing claims and practices, are being demanded by regulators as well as consumers mindful of the ethical, sustainable and environmental impacts of what they buy.

To support this new world, agricultural enterprises need to exchange verifiable data across the whole supply chain in a way that respects the ownership of the data. This involves agricultural related enterprises coming together to form an ecosystem for exchanging trusted data. This ecosystem includes, but is not limited to:

- Farms
- Banks
- Fertilizer Companies
- Meat producers
- Crop producers
- Milk producers
- Geo-Surveyors
- Wholesalers
- Government
- more

N. Dong et al. (Eds.): SDLT 2023, CCIS 1975, pp. 72–81, 2024.
https://doi.org/10.1007/978-981-97-0006-6_5

Each of these enterprises participates in the network by exchanging data in a trusted way.

This paper describes the technical implementation of a Decentralized Agricultural Ecosystem to satisfy the requirements of regulators and consumers. It takes a decentralized approach and is founded on the decentralized identity based verifiable credentials technology. It is implemented in a way to allow the data owners full control of their data and entities in the network can independently verify data they receive.

2 Implementation of a Decentralized Agricultural Ecosystem

To meet the requirements imposed on the agricultural industry a new data exchange system has been developed and implemented using decentralized identity (DI) based verifiable credentials. As shown in Fig. 1, the decentralized identity verifiable credential system involves three key parties:

- **Issuer:** This entity creates a verifiable credential holding key data and transfers it to the holder. An example of an issuer in the network would be a Green House Gas (GHG) emissions certifier.
- **Holder:** This entity requests, receives, stores, and presents the verifiable credential. A holder uses a decentralized identity wallet. An example of a holder is a farm owner.
- **Verifier:** This entity receives the verifiable credential (as a presentation proof) from the holder and is able to verify the identity of the issuer and integrity of the data. An example of a verifier is a Government department checking the GHG emissions of a farm.

Also shown is the ledger or blockchain that provides the *trust foundation* for the system.

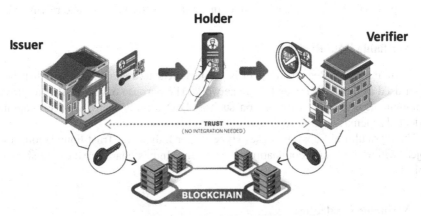

Fig. 1. The Verifiable Credential Data Exchange System

Figure 1 is also commonly called the *Triangle of Trust*. The holder (the farmer) wishes to receive a credential from the issuer (e.g. organic certifier), which they in turn present to the verifier (e.g. wholesaler).

To bootstrap the issuing of a verifiable credentials the issuer writes to the blockchain, in this case it is writing to the Hyperledger Indy network [1]. The issuer writes their Decentralized Identifier (DID) and associated information, the verifiable credential schema, and the verifiable credential definition.

The issuer is then in a position to issue verifiable credentials to the holders. The first step is to establish a DIDComm connection with the holder. Once a connection is established the issuer can present a credential issue offer to the holder. The holder then approves the offer, the verifiable credential is issued, and stored in the holder's wallet.

Once the holder has the credential it is in a position to accept a presentation proof request from a verifier. The holder (wallet) formulates the presentation proof (which could in fact be derived from multiple credentials) and delivers that to the verifier. The verifier can verify the proof by obtaining the issuer information from the blockchain. No communication is required back to the issuer.

2.1 Why Use a Decentralized Model?

Organizations want to protect their own data and share that data in a way that gives the organization more control.

Decentralization helps move the data under the stewardship of the organization to whom it belongs. Decentralization stops the direct integration between third parties. The organization is the integration point. They choose what data to share, with whom and where they want to share it, and how much of their data they want to share. That lets the organization perform the integration by following standard decentralized identity protocols.

In the Agricultural Ecosystem project the organization's data (farm data) is shared using verifiable credentials. In the issuing process the farm can receive a verifiable credential. The farm can then present that verifiable credential (presentation proof) to a relying party (verifier). There is no direct integration between issuer and relying party.

2.2 Verifiable Data Registry

The Verifiable Data Registry (VDR) is the technical term for blockchain/distributed ledger used as the *Trust Layer* for the network. The purpose of the VDR is to provide an immutable storage of information such as DIDs, public keys, service endpoints, credential schemas and so on.

The Agricultural Ecosystem uses Hyperledger Indy as its Trust Foundation. It is a project within the Linux Foundation. Hyperledger Indy's characteristics are shown in Table 1.

2.3 Verifiable Credential

Verifiable credentials are digitally signed documents that carry claims (attributes) about the subject (usually a person or organization) of the credential. For example, a plastic driver license can be re-created in a digital form as a verifiable credential. Almost any document or identity card can be made into a verifiable credential.

Table 1. Hyperledger Indy Ledger Characteristics

KEY AREA	DESCRIPTION
PUBLIC LEDGER	All data written to the ledger is open to be read by anyone
PERMISSIONED NETWORK	To write to the ledger an entity must be an approved endorser. An endorser is approved by the organization overseeing the ledger e.g. Sovrin Foundation. The endorser must agree to certain terms e.g. will not write Personally Identifiable Information (PII) to the ledger. In the Agricultural Ecosystem project each issuer is configured as an endorser. In addition, in comparison to permission-less networks, only approved validator nodes can be added to the ledger network
CONSENSUS ALGORITHM	Validator nodes on the ledger must come to agreement (consensus) before anything is written to the ledger. The Redundant Byzantine Fault Tolerance (RBFT) consensus algorithm is implemented. The size of the Hyperledger Indy network is restricted to around 24 validator nodes
GOVERNANCE	Governance is implemented in an offline and centralized way. Any changes to the governing rules is voted on through offline method, for example, by signing paper documents, rather than using on-ledger governance methods
ECONOMIC MODEL	The organization that supervises the running of the ledger e.g. Sovrin Foundation, charges for writes to the network (usually by charging an annual fee for unlimited writes)

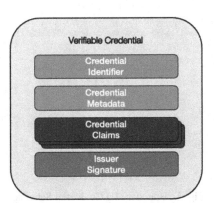

Fig. 2. Verifiable Credential Data Structure

Figure 2 shows the general form of a verifiable credential. There is an identifier and some metadata. It also holds claims that the issuer is asserting about the subject (user or organization). The issuer adds a signature to the verifiable credential so that a verifier can prove the credential's integrity.

There are significant advantages of verifiable credentials for user privacy. When the user (holder) is asked to present the credential (presentation proof) the user has control over what information is presented to the verifier. This is called selective disclosure. In addition, a Zero Knowledge Proof (ZKP) might be used which proves that a claim has a certain characteristic without revealing the claim itself. Also there is no communication between the verifier and issuer needed for the verifier to verify the credential.

The credential schema for one of the Agricultural Ecosystem credentials is shown in Fig. 3. In this case the purpose of the credential is to provide geo-spatial boundary coordinates of a farm.

```
{
  "txn": {
    "data": {
      "data": {
        "attr_names": [
          "organisation_address",
          "organisation_id",
          "satellite_image_url",
          "representative_id",
          "shape_geo_json",
          "boundary_id",
          "shape_file_url"
        ],
        "name": "Boundary_ID",
        "version": "1.0"
      }
    },
    "metadata": {
      "digest": "cbaf5ecda443ce52b66a6dd8c3b60939dfa9b39ec4b886e47ba67a898a92f653",
      "from": "QNetK7HNqt4mdmWRKGxzrZ",
      "payloadDigest": "ac7a6fe5a506103fd1cb4b7f8305453415b983b53bb4b5b13d6edddd915fe820",
      "reqId": 1686744132940649200,
      "taaAcceptance": {
        "mechanism": "wallet_agreement",
        "taaDigest": "c965dd01fec099ea95babaea3031bc09905432d3d7f1519bc0b99971aece8592",
        "time": 1686700800
      },
      "protocolVersion": 2,
      "type": "101",
      "typeName": "SCHEMA"
    },
    "txnMetadata": {
      "seqNo": 45461,
      "txnId": "QNetK7HNqt4mdmWRKGxzrZ:2:Boundary_ID:1.0",
      "txnTime": "2023-06-14T12:02:12.000Z"
    }
  }
}
```

Fig. 3. Boundary ID Credential Schema

2.4   AnonCreds vs W3C Credentials

There are two main types of verifiable credentials associated with the Agricultural Ecosystem project today.

The AnonCreds [2] or anonymous credentials specification created as part of the Hyperledger AnonCreds Project. AnonCreds are very commonly used for verifiable credentials projects. Some advantages of AnonCreds based credentials:

- Anonymity—The credential itself does not contain the identifier of the subject of the credential. A technology called link secret allows the holder of the credential to prove they were issued the credential without revealing their identity.
- Revocation—An issuer is able to revoke a credential in real time. The next time that (revoked) credential is presented to a verifier the verification will fail.
- Reduced PII exposure—Implementation of both selective disclosure and zero knowledge proofs assists in protecting the privacy of the credential subject.

An alternative credential type has been created by the World Wide Web Consortium (W3C). This new credential format has been defined in the Verifiable Credentials Data Model v1.1. [3]. This W3C recommendation is particularly of interest to government applications.

There are a few limitations in W3C credentials in comparison to AnonCreds:

- Anonymity—It is the normal practice with W3C credentials for the subject identifier (usually subject DID) to be placed within the credential itself.
- Revocation—The W3C data model does not specifically include a revocation process.
- Reduced PII exposure—To obtain the benefits of selective disclosure and ZKPs, a W3C credential has to be created in that way e.g. using the signature types that support it. It is not the default for W3C credentials.

The project has initially used AnonCreds as the credential standard. However, due to government regulation the use of W3C verifiable credentials is on the roadmap to potentially replace AnonCreds.

2.5 Connections, Issuing, Presentation Proof Protocols

The initial protocols implemented in the Agricultural Ecosystem follow the RFCs as part of the Aries Interop Protocol (AIP) 1.0 [4].

A holder (wallet) makes a DIDComm connection - the initial implementation follows Aries RFC 0160: Connection Protocol [5] - with the issuer.

The verifiable credential - the initial implementation follows Aries RFC 0036: Issue Credential Protocol 1.0 [6] - is sent over the connection and stored in the holder's wallet.

The holder in turn establishes a new DIDComm connection to the relying party (verifier). The verifier requests a proof presentation - the initial implementation uses Aries RFC 0037: Present Proof Protocol 1.0 [7] – and receives that from the holder.

As the project moves to use W3C credentials then the AIP 1.0 protocols will be replaced with the AIP 2.0 protocols (at least for issue and presentation proof) [8], a requirement for using the W3C credentials.

2.6 Governance

In a Decentralized Agriculture Ecosystem there is a centralized authority for making and enforcing the rules of the network. The participants therefore agree to follow a set rules for the network.

Some examples of the governance rules related to verifiable credentials:

- What is the list of trusted issuers in the network?
- What credentials are those trusted issuers allowed to issue?
- What is the list of trusted verifiers in the network?
- What credentials are the allowed to verify?

There are two main standards for enforcing governance within the network:

- Trust Registry [9]: When an event occurs, for example, a wallet receives a credential offer from an issuer, the wallet makes a call to a central server to query whether the offer is obeying the governance rules.
- Machine Readable Governance [10, 11]: In this case a JSON file is created that describes the rules and is distributed to every participant in the network. That is,the JSON file is distributed to all issuers, verifiers and holders (wallets).

Within the Agricultural Ecosystem, the decision was made to follow the Machine Readable Governance approach. The network coordinator creates a JSON file with the rules and this is distributed to each participant (Issuers, Holders, Verifiers) in the network.

2.7 Decentralized Identity Wallet

A decentralized identity wallet is an application that allows a person to receive, store and present verifiable credentials that relate to them. Examples of the type of credentials that a person might receive into their personal DI wallet are passport, vaccine certificates, club memberships, flight tickets and access credentials. The personal DI wallet allows secure connections to be established with verifiable credential issuers and verifiers, and for the requesting, receiving, storing and presenting of verifiable credentials and for secure communication. It also allows secure connections to be made with another user's personal DI wallet to allow for secure communication between the users.

There are a number of personal DI wallets in existence, such as created by Lissi, Trinsic, Indicio, and Anonyome Labs and they are typically mobile or desktop applications. They are relatively easy to install and use by normal users. In the Agricultural Ecosystem we have used the Anonyome Labs personal DI wallet as shown in Fig. 4. In the figure the wallet is shown with five of the credentials used in the project.

The farming credentials are not restricted to only text based claims. On the left of Fig. 5 is the credential for a Green House Gas (GHG) certificate for a farm. In this example a PDF link is included in the credential. The wallet is then able to present the PDF. On the right of Fig. 5 is another credential showing the geographic boundary of the farm. In this case the credential includes the coordinates of the farm as one of the claims. The wallet is then able to present the graphical image of the farm by interpreting those coordinates.

2.8 Personal vs Enterprise Decentralized Identity Wallets

In projects such as the Agricultural Ecosystem, the use of personal DI wallets are increasingly seen as too limited. This current generation of personal DI wallets do not provide

Fig. 4. Credentials from the Agricultural Ecosystem project

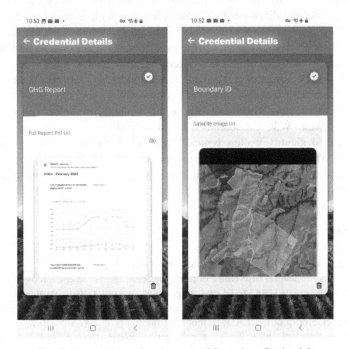

Fig. 5. Green House Gas Report and Boundary Credentials

sufficient capability for business or government use. In these settings a new type of wallet is required, that provides capabilities above and beyond a personal DI wallet.

To begin with, this new wallet (which we will call the enterprise DI wallet) does **NOT** hold verifiable credentials representing PII from an individual. Instead the enterprise DI wallet holds verifiable credentials that are representative of data related to the enterprise. For example, a verifiable credential in an enterprise DI wallet might represent a farm's GHG emission certificate. Or it might represent the organic status of a farm. The data may be sensitive from a privacy/business confidentiality point of view, but more importantly the integrity of data needs to be verifiable.

Another difference between a personal DI wallet and an enterprise DI wallet is that in the personal DI wallet, usually only the person (whose PII data is contained in the verifiable credentials in the wallet) accesses it. Whereas the enterprise DI wallet may need to be accessible by more than one authorized employee of the enterprise requiring a delegated authorization model to provide selective user access to the enterprise DI wallet.

Although the initial phase of the project used a personal DI wallet, the proposal is to replace this with an enterprise DI wallet.

3   Conclusions

The decentralized identity verifiable credential system provides an excellent foundation for providing a decentralized verifiable data exchange. This is possible because every part of the decentralized identity verifiable credentials system is standardized: DIDs, verifiable credentials, issuer-holder-verifier protocols, verifiable data registry and so on.

Participants in the Agricultural Ecosystem therefore choose roles of issuer, verifier or holder and can exchange data following these standards. It has also been possible to build this system with a consortium of different software vendors each following the standards. The network will need to evolve as the standards preferences change, such as the desire to move to W3C Credentials from AnonCreds.

Decentralized identity wallets typically are built for individual users and not for organizations. This has highlighted the need for an enterprise DI wallet, one that is built to share organizational data, and one that is accessible by multiple administrators of the organization.

References

1. Hyperledger Indy. https://www.hyperledger.org/projects/hyperledger-indy
2. AnonCreds Specification v1.0 Draft. https://hyperledger.github.io/anoncreds-spec/
3. Verifiable Credentials Data Model v1.1. https://www.w3.org/TR/vc-data-model/
4. Aries Interop Protocol 1.0. https://github.com/hyperledger/aries-rfcs/blob/main/concepts/0302-aries-interop-profile/README.md#aries-interop-profile-version-10
5. Connection Protocol. https://github.com/hyperledger/aries-rfcs/tree/4d9775490359e234ab8d1c152bca6f534e92a38d/features/0160-connection-protocol
6. Issue Credential Protocol 1.0 Aries RFC0036. https://github.com/hyperledger/aries-rfcs/tree/bb42a6c35e0d5543718fb36dd099551ab192f7b0/features/0036-issue-credential

7. Presentation Proof Protocol 1.0 Aries RFC0037. https://github.com/hyperledger/aries-rfcs/tree/4fae574c03f9f1013db30bf2c0c676b1122f7149/features/0037-present-proof

8. Aries Interop Protocol 2.0. https://github.com/hyperledger/aries-rfcs/blob/main/concepts/0302-aries-interop-profile/README.md#aries-interop-profile-version-20

9. ToIP Trust Registry Specification. https://wiki.trustoverip.org/display/HOME/ToIP+Trust+Registry+Protocol+Specification

10. Trust Establishment 1.0. https://identity.foundation/trust-establishment/

11. Credential Trust Establishment. https://identity.foundation/credential-trust-establishment/

Linking NFT Transaction Events to Identify Privacy Risks

Dorottya Zelenyanszki[1(✉)], Zhé Hóu[1(✉)], Kamanashis Biswas[2(✉)], and Vallipuram Muthukkumarasamy[1(✉)]

[1] Griffith University, Brisbane, Australia
{dorottya.zelenyanszki,z.hou,v.muthu}@griffithuni.edu.au
[2] Australian Catholic University, Brisbane, Australia
kamanashis.biswas@acu.edu.au

Abstract. Non-fungible tokens (NFTs) are unique tokens with various domains, e.g. real estate, metaverse, gaming and public auctions. However, when minted on public blockchains, the underlying blockchain transaction data can be publicly accessible. This instigated transaction data analysis for various purposes, including cryptocurrency price prediction and NFT market analysis. The public data may be considered privacy-sensitive which sets a barrier to the wider adoption of NFTs. In this work, we present that the analysis of the transaction events can describe activities in NFT applications by establishing connections between transactions and thereby, it can identify information that may be privacy-sensitive. This can be useful in developing suitable privacy-enhancing methods for NFTs. We collected transaction data from a blockchain-based game called Planet IX that was built on the Polygon blockchain and used graph visualisation to provide examples for constructed connections.

Keywords: blockchain · non-fungible tokens · privacy · data analysis

1 Introduction

Public blockchains provide a decentralised and secure environment to build decentralised applications (dApps). Those applications often involve NFTs, which introduce multiple use cases for these tokens, such as metaverse objects, game items, art and tickets [10]. As NFTs can represent any unique item, the number of application areas may potentially grow. Public blockchains are accessible by anyone, and transaction data has been presented to be utilised to analyse blockchain activities [11]. Transactions include multiple pieces of information that can be considered privacy sensitive, such as wallet addresses and transacted values, and it can also be linked to other transactions and from that, even more connecting data can be extracted. This can lead to a number of potential privacy issues such as de-anonymization, transaction fingerprinting or transaction pattern exposure [3].

Several technologies such as zero-knowledge proofs (ZKPs) [5–9] and differential privacy [8] have been applied to enhance the privacy of blockchain-based

N. Dong et al. (Eds.): SDLT 2023, CCIS 1975, pp. 82–97, 2024.
https://doi.org/10.1007/978-981-97-0006-6_6

applications. The identification of the privacy-critical NFT-related information can enable the development of improved, more application-specific privacy-enhancing techniques because a more detailed picture of the application's privacy situation is provided.

Previous studies also conducted research on blockchain transaction analysis, including data related to NFTs. However, these mainly focus on network evolution analysis [13], anomaly/vulnerability detection [4], cryptocurrency price prediction [6] or NFT market analysis [2]. However, there is a potential for dApps that involve social interactions, such as multiple players in games or interactions between avatars in the virtual worlds of metaverses. NFTs are highly suitable for these types of applications as they can represent the users but also the digital objects they are interacting with.

In the submitted transactions of the dApps, multiple events are also emitted. These events also include information that potentially can be sensitive or can be utilised to link multiple events or transactions, and by that, additional information can be revealed, which then can lead to the construction of behavioural patterns of the dApp's user base. Their analysis, therefore, can lay down a foundation for identifying the privacy-sensitive NFT-related data which then can prompt the introduction of updated privacy-preserving methods. Although, our focus is the NFTs, the analysis of the events is general and not restricted to our NFT scope.

In order to conduct the analysis, we collected transactions from a blockchain-based game that includes NFTs called Planet IX[1] which runs on the Polygon PoS[2], which is an Ethereum scalability solution. We extracted the basic transaction information and the event logs, and we categorised both the event types and properties. We also used graph visualisation to show how events can connect to other events in different transactions. Finally, we also discussed how the combination of these can be utilised for the detection of privacy-critical information.

The rest of the paper is structured as follows: Sect. 2 introduces related works to this research. Following that, in Sect. 3 we give a high-level overview of the concept that describes how we analyse blockchain transaction logs. In Sect. 4 we explain how the data collection has been conducted. In Sect. 5 we discuss in detail how we analysed the data, present some visualisation results and describe what the results can be used in regards to NFT privacy. Finally, in Sect. 6 we conclude the paper and mention our planned future steps to enhance this research.

2   Related Works

This section presents the related research works. It provides examples of both blockchain-based analysis and previously used privacy-enhancing techniques and also describes where this research offers an enhancement in this area.

Zhao et al. [13] described the Ethereum blockchain as an ecosystem that consists of users and contracts that cohabit with the blockchain fabric. It is not like

---

[1]   https://planetix.com/.
[2]   https://polygon.technology/.

an online social network or a financial network; it is more like the Internet where users and programs interact with each other based on predefined rules. They aimed to study Ethereum by examining all interactions (user-to-user, user-to-contract, contract-to-user, contract-to-contract) in order to explore the evolution of the network, its properties and communities. To achieve this, they constructed four temporal networks from Ethereum and they applied global network properties to detect changes and anomalies. They also leveraged machine learning models to make predictions regarding the continuation of the determined communities. They presented that these techniques can be applied in areas such as blockchain intelligence and blockchain-based social networks.

Hu et al. [4] stated that classification could help identify smart contract vulnerabilities because contracts have different behavioural characteristics and application use cases, which show a variance in their detection. The classification can potentially also rely on the deployer of a contract because it can reveal the true purpose of the contract and it can also consider the identified design issues because they can potentially consume a large amount of gas. For this purpose, they manually analysed 10,000 smart contracts. They identified 4 behaviour patterns, and 14 basic features and also designed a data-slicing approach to minimalise the negative effect of insufficient datasets, which enabled them to present the effectiveness of the approach in an LSTM network.

Casale-Brunet et al. [2] mentioned that there can be a parallel drawn between NFT transaction graphs and graphs that are used to describe social media interactions. The latter has been previously used to determine user preferences, and they stated that there is a possibility that related algorithms can be leveraged to identify trusted/influential wallets and analyse market evolution. To explore this area, a systematic analysis has been conducted on the evolution of the NFT communities based on their interaction graphs and related properties. This analysis presented results in identifying so-called super nodes, which are wallets that coexist in multiple NFT collections and that have been presented to be influential on the market.

Wan et al. [9] mentioned that smart contracts take off-chain data as input through interactions. They also added that it is highly important to provide data authenticity and privacy protection for the off-chain data. Their research on existing works presented that they only offer a solution for either of those; therefore, to provide an enhancement on this, they designed an extended zero-knowledge succinct non-interactive argument of knowledge (zk-SNARK) called zk-DASNARK that handles the data authentication by also leveraging digital signatures. Their model, a zero-knowledge authenticated data feed system (zk-AuthFeed) utilises zk-DASNARK to provide data authentication and privacy protection for dApps.

Huang et al. [5] focused on data availability in decentralised storage such as blockchain. They proposed a data integrity checking protocol. This protocol uses efficient verifiable delay functions (EVDF), Fiat-Shamir ZKPs, Merkle trees and smart contracts to offer this functionality. This way, they presented a protocol that does not leak important information, ensures fairness among participants and provides public verification.

These works showed that blockchain-related data analysis may include research on the evolution of communities, but it does not cover in-depth analysis of the user activities that are occurring in the dApps. We state that the events emitted in blockchain transactions can describe user activities within the applications, including giving a picture of the situation regarding the privacy-critical information that is shared. This can be facilitated by introducing similar upgraded privacy-preserving techniques to [5–9] that are based on specific privacy-sensitive information identified by the transaction events analysis. It can also lay down a foundation for user behaviour analysis by leveraging techniques used for similar purposes in social networks. Similar to how Adali et al. [1] constructed new behavioural features to understand user behaviour on Twitter or how Yang et al. [12] utilised factor graph model to make predictions in regards to retweeting behaviour.

Table 1. Basic collected features

Name	Description
blockHash	Unique block identifier
blockNumber	Number of the block the transaction occurred in
transactionHash	Unique transaction identifier
timestamp	Date and time
from	Sender address
to	Receiver address
value	Value of the transaction
isError	Whether any error occurred during execution (boolean)
txreceipt status	Transaction execution status message
contractAddress	Smart contract address
methodId	Transaction method identifier
input	Transaction input data

3   Overview of the Proposed Concept

This section presents the proposed concept for identifying privacy-critical information. It is divided into three phases: data collection, visualisation through graphs and analysis, and the concept can be seen in Fig. 1. In the following, we describe each step and also refer to the section where they are described in detail.

3.1   Data Collection Phase

At first, transaction data has to be extracted from the application's underlying blockchain through publicly available APIs. The dApps have one or multiple

smart contracts that handle their activities. Therefore, for sufficient data collection, it is advised to extract data from multiple contracts. Need to highlight
that it is also important to collect data that belongs to the same timeframe
as this data going to be leveraged to describe user activities over time later.
From that transaction data, basic features (detailed in Table 1) that are already
used in blockchain analysis (e.g. wallet addresses) are extracted, and the transaction's event logs are also decoded. This data is then converted into a CSV
format which is suitable for establishing the graph visualisation later. The data
collection phase is described in detail in Sect. 4.2.

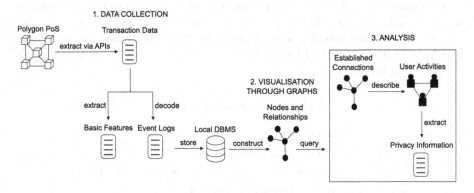

Fig. 1. Overview of the proposed method.

3.2   Visualisation Through Graphs Phase

From the converted CSV files, multiple graph nodes and relationships are constructed as described in Sect. 5.1. These are then stored in a local database.
Using the nodes and relationships the collected data can be queried to establish connections between distinct blockchain data that would not be connected
by default. We provided examples for these in Sect. 5.2. These examples show
how a single event property can link multiple transactions including ones that
happened at different time points as they belong to differing blocks. If an event
property type and value pair has the ability to establish connections to a high
number of events that belong to other transactions, then we can consider it
privacy-critical. Identifying these critical pairs is the first step towards using
this concept to describe the privacy of NFTs.

3.3   Analysis Phase

These connections can be leveraged to describe user activities within the application over time which can eventually also reveal the privacy information that
is leaked through events and has to be protected through specifically designed
novel privacy-enhancing techniques as the analysis of these connections gives a

picture of the application from a privacy point of view. We also plan to use these connections to construct general privacy patterns so we can leverage established techniques from social network analysis to add a more general classification of privacy-sensitive NFT-related data in dApps. These patterns can describe certain NFT activities or attacks.

4   Data Collection and Processing

In order to present the significance of the concept proposed in the previous section, a small data collection and analysis have been conducted. In this section, we describe the tools we utilised for this purpose and also present how the data collection was performed.

Table 2. Event types

Type	Description	Example
log	Log events of application activities	LogFeeTransfer
mint	Mint events	PIXMinted
NFT	Certain NFT-related events	NFTPlaced
token	Events that cover tokens	TokenClaimed
transfer	Transfer events	Transfer
staking	Staking related events	TokenStaked
other	Every other type of events e.g. application-specific events	Combined

Table 3. Event property type groups

Group	Description	Example
app	App-related properties	operator, approved
log	Properties of log events	input1, output1
user	Properties with address value	account, user
id	Id properties	pixId
token	Token-related properties	tokenId, tokenAddress
value	Value properties	amount
staking	Staking properties	stakeable
other	Other properties e.g. application-specific events	location (x, y)

4.1   Experimental Setup

We conducted the experiment on macOS 13.2.1 and used Python 3.9.6 to run scripts to extract blockchain transaction data and convert it into a suitable CSV format. For analysis and visualisation, the Neo4j Desktop $1.5.8^3$ was utilised where we established a local DBMS 1.5.8 to store the data that can be used for this. To perform queries, we also added the extended APOC library[4].

4.2 Data Collection

Transaction data has been extracted from three smart contract addresses of Planet IX. The first one is the contract for the PIX NFT[5] which is a hexagon-shaped virtual copy of a part of the planet Earth that users can own in this game. The second contract is for Mission Control[6] where the users can stake their NFT assets such as PIX NFTs. The third and final contract is for Gravity Grade[7], which is an in-game corporation through which the users can obtain fresh PIXs [7]. We collected 1000 transactions from each address between the block numbers 43845596 and 46574022, thereby enabling us to see user activities within the same time period. In the future, more transactions can be extracted from these addresses, and more addresses from the game can be involved to present a picture of user activities on a larger time period and on a wider scale of the application.

To obtain transactions and their events, we used PolygonScan API[8] and the Polygon PoS API on Alchemy[9]. For each transaction, some basic features have been extracted, and the event logs have also been decoded. The basic features can be seen in Table 1. Since every included smart contract address uses the EIP-1967 Transparent Proxy pattern[10], we had to obtain the implementation address first in order to get the correct contract ABI, which is required to decode the event logs. Both the basic features and the decoded logs for each transaction were placed into a JSON file. We also extracted each address and implementation address and put it into a separate JSON file so we could use it later for filtering purposes.

After this step, we went through the transactions again and checked whether they had any decoded event logs associated with them. If yes, we categorised each event into one of the event types presented in Table 2, and we also grouped all the event properties into groups presented in Table 3. The types and the groups were assigned based on the event and property names. This is the reason for having both NFT and token event types; as for the latter, it is not certain that it is NFT-related because the game includes other types of tokens as well. Although it can be assumed to be the same NFT token. We plan to use these types and groups for the analysis of other applications as well; therefore, eventually, they are going to be generalised. We also assigned unique IDs for both the events and

---

[3] https://neo4j.com/.

[4] https://neo4j.com/labs/apoc/5/.

[5] https://polygonscan.com/address/0xb2435253c71fca27be41206eb2793e44e1df6b6d.

[6] https://polygonscan.com/address/0x24e541a5c32830a4e8b89846fd4bf86e294dd3cb.

[7] https://polygonscan.com/address/0x3376c61c450359d402f07909bda979a4c0e6c32f.

[8] https://docs.polygonscan.com/.

[9] https://docs.alchemy.com/reference/polygon-api-quickstart.

[10] https://eips.ethereum.org/EIPS/eip-1967.

their event property type and value pairs so they can be easily queried later. We also collected every unique event property type and value pair separately as they are often repeated in subsequent events. We extracted three separate CSV files from this process: one for the events, one for all the event property types and value pairs and one for every unique event property type and value pairs.

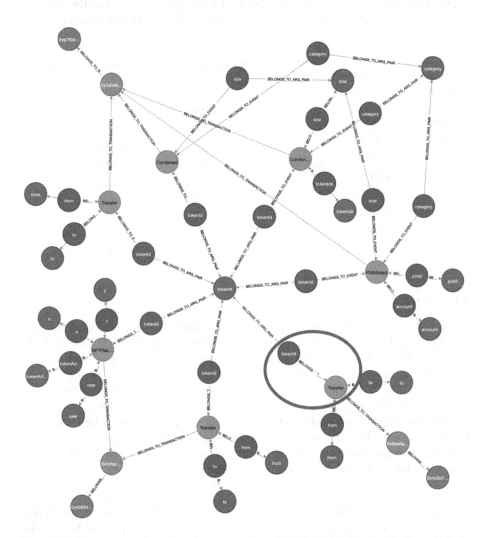

Fig. 2. Linking transactions based on one event which is highlighted with the red circle (Color figure online)

5   Analysis and Discussion

The collected, categorised data in CSV format enabled us to visualise the user activities in a graph format. This not only allowed us to present them in an easy-to-understand form but also presented how to connect multiple pieces of information initiated from only one event. In this section, we describe how we established the DBMS in Neo4j and present the results in the discussion section.

Table 4. Number of connecting events per event property type and value pair group

Group	# connecting events
user	3012534122
other	371951778
id	58806468
token	17231980
value	1106028
staking	774080

Table 5. Number of connecting events per event type

Type	# connecting events
transfer	3011980562
mint	224203980
other	216506850
nft+token	9713064
staking	0

5.1   Neo4j Setup

In order to visualise the data from the data collection, we introduced 6 types of nodes and 4 types of relationships based on the 4 types of CSV files for each contract address. Note that events with a log type and property type and value pairs with an app or log group have been discarded during the import to the DBMS. The log events and properties have been excluded because they do not offer new information. They usually log event data that has been previously emitted through other events such as when an approval event is emitted after a transfer event. The app properties have been neglected because our focus is on user activities that can lead to identifying privacy-sensitive information that relates to the NFTs. We describe them as follows:

Nodes:

1. Block(blockHash, blockNumber, timeStamp): This refers to the blocks in the blockchain that can be identified by the unique block hash or by the blockNumber. They include multiple transactions, and they also determine the date and time for all those transactions by the timestamp. Blocks are represented by purple colour.
2. Transaction(transactionHash, blockHash, fromAddr, toAddr, methodId, value): This refers to the transactions in the blockchain identified by their transaction hashes. It also has block hashes as properties to identify which block the transactions belong to. The other properties are a subset of the basic

features from Table 1. Transactions can emit events as well. Transactions are represented by orange colour.

3. Event(uuid, event, type, transactionHash): This node describes the events that are emitted through transactions that are determined by their assigned unique IDs. It also includes properties for the name of the event and its categorised type. The transaction the event belongs to can be extracted by the included transaction hash. Events are represented by light-blue colour.

4. Arg(uuid, argType, argValue, group, eventUuid): This node determines all the event property type and value pairs. They are all identified by a preassigned unique ID and also include a property for the group they belong to. The event in which they have been emitted is determined by the eventUuid property. Property pairs are represented by dark-blue colour.

5. ArgPair(argType, argValue, group): Some event property types and value pairs are repeating across multiple events from differing transactions and blocks. This node refers to every unique pair. Unique property pairs are represented by red colour.

6. Contract(address): This node describes every contract and implementation address that has been deducted from decoding the events. These nodes are used for filtering. Contracts are represented by green colour, although, they are never part of the resulting graph of the query.

Relationships:

1. BELONGS_TO_BLOCK: This relationship returns with transaction and block pairs where the transaction has been submitted to the blockchain within that particular block.

2. BELONGS_TO_TRANSACTION: This relationship returns with event and transaction pairs where the event has been emitted through that particular transaction.

3. BELONGS_TO_EVENT: This relationship returns with the event property type and value pair and event pairs where the event property belongs to that particular event.

4. BELONGS_TO_ARG_PAIR: This presents how event property type and value pairs can repeat throughout multiple events. The relationship shows that every pair belongs to a unique pair.

5.2 Visualising Through Graph Format

The established nodes and relationships can be utilised to query the collected data. Note that the results of the queries have been limited in order to present graphs that have a number of nodes and edges that make the resulting graphs still visually pleasing but also show how can we link NFT-related information.

Case Study: Location Data Leakage. In Fig. 2 we present an example of how multiple events, transactions and blocks can be connected even through

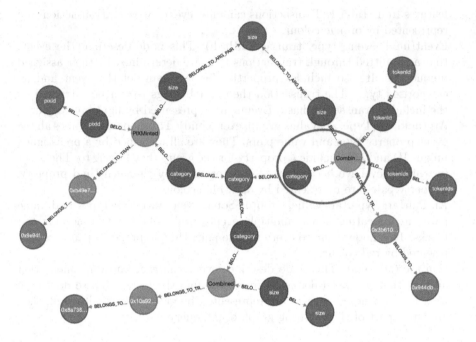

Fig. 3. Linking transactions through an event property pair that belongs to the other group (Color figure online)

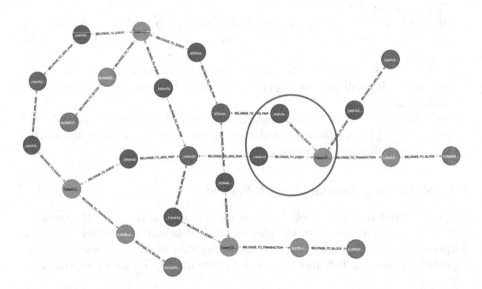

Fig. 4. Linking transactions based on an event that belongs to the token type (Color figure online)

one event. We take a simple Transfer event and its tokenId property (high-lighted with the red coloured circle). By using the BELONGS_TO_ARG_PAIR relation, we identify the unique property pair (displayed at the centre of the figure) that connects the first event to other events. In this case, this pair is the previously mentioned tokenId event property and its value. By leveraging the other relations, we also present that with this query we cover three points in time because the connecting transactions belong to three different blocks. This suggests that through the analysis of the event logs, we can present what sort of activities the event property pairs are involved in over time. This can be utilised for various types of use cases including providing NFT life-cycle information. We also displayed every event's other properties and which unique pairs they belong to. This can reveal additional information about the highlighted event property pair. For example, the connecting NFTPlaced event has the x and y properties, which gives location information for that particular NFT in the game at that particular point in time. This NFT is identified by the token address included in the NFTPlaced event and by the tokenId through which the two events are connected. Information revealed in this way can be potentially privacy-sensitive. For example, in a metaverse setting a piece of similar location information can reveal where the participant's NFT avatars are located within the virtual world, which can be highly useful for malicious actors who try to introduce behavioural patterns of victim users so they can commit user-specific malevolent actions. The query to construct this graph is the following:

```
MATCH (c:Contract)
MATCH r1=(a1:Arg)-[:BELONGS_TO_EVENT]->(e1:Event), r2=(
    a1)-[:BELONGS_TO_ARG_PAIR]->(p:ArgPair), r3=(e1)-[:
    BELONGS_TO_TRANSACTION]->(t1:Transaction), r4=(t1)
    -[:BELONGS_TO_BLOCK]->(b1:Block), r5=(a2:Arg)-[:
    BELONGS_TO_EVENT]->(e1), r6=(a2:Arg)-[:
    BELONGS_TO_ARG_PAIR]->(), r7=(a3:Arg)-[:
    BELONGS_TO_ARG_PAIR]->(p), r8=(a3)-[:
    BELONGS_TO_EVENT]->(e2:Event), r9=(a4:Arg)-[:
    BELONGS_TO_EVENT]->(e2), r10=(a4)-[:
    BELONGS_TO_ARG_PAIR]-(), r11=(e2)-[:
    BELONGS_TO_TRANSACTION]->(t2:Transaction), r12=(t2)
    -[:BELONGS_TO_BLOCK]->(b2:Block) WHERE NOT a1 = a2
    AND NOT a3 = a4 AND NOT e1 = e2 AND NOT toLower(p.
    argValue) = toLower(c.address)
RETURN r1,r2,r3,r4,r5,r6,r7,r8,r9,r10,r11,r12
LIMIT 400
```

Filtering Using Types and Groups. We can also use the event types and event property pair groups to provide similar graphs to show the linking of infor-mation. For example, in Fig. 3 we see how we can connect events through an event that has an event property pair that is part of the other group which probably means that it is an application-specific property. In that figure, we highlighted the initiating CombinedWithBurned event and the connecting category property pair with a red coloured circle. In Fig. 4 we take an event that specifically belongs to the token type. This results in a graph where multiple TokenClaimed events connect through multiple property pairs. Within the red circle, we can see how events either connect through the tokenId or through the stakeable property pair from the initiating event's point of view. But two of them also connect via another separate userAddress property pair as well. These types of queries can be leveraged to describe the privacy influence level of certain events and property groups which can eventually help us filter out certain events that have negligible importance in describing user activities. The queries for these graphs are identical to the previously listed query, but they have an additional condition for either the type or the group. For example, the query for Fig. 3 is as follows:

```
MATCH (c:Contract)
MATCH r1=(a1:Arg)-[:BELONGS_TO_EVENT]->(e1:Event), r2=(a1)-[:
    BELONGS_TO_ARG_PAIR]->(p:ArgPair), r3=(e1)-[:
    BELONGS_TO_TRANSACTION]->(t1:Transaction), r4=(t1)-[:
    BELONGS_TO_BLOCK]->(b1:Block), r5=(a2:Arg)-[:BELONGS_TO_EVENT
    ]->(e1), r6=(a2:Arg)-[:BELONGS_TO_ARG_PAIR]->(), r7=(a3:Arg)-[:
    BELONGS_TO_ARG_PAIR]->(p), r8=(a3)-[:BELONGS_TO_EVENT]->(e2:
    Event), r9=(a4:Arg)-[:BELONGS_TO_EVENT]->(e2), r10=(a4)-[:
    BELONGS_TO_ARG_PAIR]-(), r11=(e2)-[:BELONGS_TO_TRANSACTION]->(t2
    :Transaction), r12=(t2)-[:BELONGS_TO_BLOCK]->(b2:Block) WHERE
    NOT a1 = a2 AND NOT a3 = a4 AND NOT e1 = e2 AND NOT toLower(p.
    argValue) = toLower(c.address) AND p.group = "other"
RETURN r1,r2,r3,r4,r5,r6,r7,r8,r9,r10,r11,r12
LIMIT 80
```

5.3   Discussion

In order to understand what NFT-related information is privacy-sensitive, at first, we have to determine what type of information has the ability to establish multiple connections that can describe user activities and eventually user behaviour which can then enable us to leverage techniques that are used in social networks for user analysis.

The event types and event property pair groups can be leveraged for this purpose. Through a simple query, we can check which type and group has the highest number of connecting events. Note that at this stage we take the NFT and token events together as there is a need for additional data in order to determine how to differentiate them completely. Table 4 and 5 present that in general events are connected through a pair that belongs to either the user or other group and the connecting events are usually transfer, mint or other events. As the staking group provided the least connecting pairs and there were no staking events that made a connection, we can assume that staking does not have a significant influence on determining user activities which means that it can be potentially filtered out.

Although this presents the user group and the transfer events as major connectors, when we look into the event properties of the connecting events, we can see that the user, other and token groups are all able to make connections to event properties from five different groups. The exact numbers can be seen in Table 6. We assume that the underwhelming influence of the user group comes from the fact that 6981 events out of 8518 total events are transfer events that usually involve wallet address properties that belong to the user group.

This proves that events can be connected through multiple types of properties and via these connecting event property types and value pairs we can associate information with information that automatically would not be assumed. For example, it is clear that an NFT has a tokenId and an owner just by using the underlying smart contract; however, application-specific information such as its category, ID or location may not be part of its metadata (which can be extracted by the contract) or transactions events submitted by its contract. Therefore, an event property that has high connection ability can be declared as information that has a high influence on privacy as it will establish connections to a high number of differing event properties which enhances the richness of the described user activities which then enables us to eventually reveal an increased number of privacy-critical NFT-related information. In order to lay down the foundation for user activity analysis, more application data has to be extracted from the blockchain as we need a greater variety of events so we can establish event property groups and event types that are more specific.

Table 6. Number of connecting events categorised by the group of their connecting property pair

Group	# connecting events	
user	user	1505161855
	token	1505532427
	id	609708
	value	249852
	other	980280
other	user	41746605
	token	165294690
	id	41045067
	staking	54096
	other	123811320
token	user	1111067
	token	5436129
	id	4368
	staking	53256
	other	10627160
id	user	14801472
	token	14641704
	value	79884
	other	29283408
value	user	737352
	id	368676
staking	token	387040
	other	387040

6   Conclusion

The lack of privacy of the NFTs is one of the major obstacles to applying them on a wider application scale. The information revealed through transactions (e.g. addresses, value) can be considered privacy-sensitive; therefore, it needs some type of privacy-enhancing technique to be utilised to protect it. We also argue that the event logs emitted in the transaction can cause further privacy leakage and it can be also utilised to link multiple transactions. In this research, we presented how transactions from a chosen application can be extracted and then how their events can be decoded and utilised to establish connections between information pieces that by definition may not be connected. We argue that by establishing these connections, user activities of dApps can be extracted which is the first step to identifying the privacy-critical NFT-related information in dApps which can eventually lead to the establishment of user behavioural patterns. We also used graph-based visualisation to present examples of the connections. The analysis of blockchain transaction events can also enable the development of novel privacy-enhancing techniques that are based on the identified privacy-critical NFT-related data.

In our future work, we will collect more data from the already mentioned smart contracts and include additional contracts from the application. This will enable us to refine the event types and groups and show a wide variety of user activities in a longer time period. User activities may be analysed to identify the privacy-sensitive information. This may reveal various types of issues and vulnerabilities in regard to the NFTs and their end-users. By leveraging already established social network analysis techniques we also plan to introduce general privacy patterns which may then be utilised to introduce effective methods for privacy protection. More experiments may be performed with a different dApp to validate the results from the first instalment.

References

1. Adali, S., Golbeck, J.: Predicting personality with social behavior. In: 2012 IEEE/ACM International Conference on Advances in Social Networks Analysis and Mining, pp. 302–309 (2012). https://doi.org/10.1109/ASONAM.2012.58
2. Casale-Brunet, S., Ribeca, P., Doyle, P., Mattavelli, M.: Networks of Ethereum non-fungible tokens: a graph-based analysis of the ERC-721 ecosystem. In: 2021 IEEE International Conference on Blockchain (Blockchain), pp. 188–195. IEEE Computer Society, Los Alamitos (2021). https://doi.org/10.1109/Blockchain53845.2021.00033
3. Feng, Q., He, D., Zeadally, S., Khan, M.K., Kumar, N.: A survey on privacy protection in blockchain system. J. Netw. Comput. Appl. **126**, 45–58 (2019). https://doi.org/10.1016/j.jnca.2018.10.020, https://www.sciencedirect.com/science/article/pii/S1084804518303485
4. Hu, T., et al.: Transaction-based classification and detection approach for Ethereum smart contract. Inf. Proc. Manage. **58**(2), 102462 (2021). https://doi.org/10.1016/j.ipm.2020.102462, https://www.sciencedirect.com/science/article/pii/S0306457320309547
5. Huang, Y., Yu, Y., Li, H., Li, Y., Tian, A.: Blockchain-based continuous data integrity checking protocol with zero-knowledge privacy protection. Digit. Commun. Netw. **8**(5), 604–613 (2022). https://doi.org/10.1016/j.dcan.2022.04.017, https://www.sciencedirect.com/science/article/pii/S2352864822000669
6. Ozer, F., Sakar, C.O.: An automated cryptocurrency trading system based on the detection of unusual price movements with a time-series clustering-based approach. Expert Syst. Appl. **200**, 117017 (2022). https://doi.org/10.1016/j.eswa.2022.117017, https://www.sciencedirect.com/science/article/pii/S0957417422004353

7. Software, N.: Whitepaper (2022). https://planetix.gitbook.io/whitepaper/. Accessed 3 Aug 2023

8. Ul Hassan, M., Rehmani, M.H., Chen, J.: Differential privacy in blockchain technology: a futuristic approach. J. Parallel Distrib. Comput. **145**, 50–74 (2020). https://doi.org/10.1016/j.jpdc.2020.06.003, https://www.sciencedirect.com/science/article/pii/S0743731520303105

9. Wan, Z., Zhou, Y., Ren, K.: zk-AuthFeed: protecting data feed to smart contracts with authenticated zero knowledge proof. IEEE Trans. Dependable Secure Comput. **20**(2), 1335–1347 (2023). https://doi.org/10.1109/TDSC.2022.3153084

10. Wang, Q., Li, R., Wang, Q., Chen, S.: Non-fungible token (NFT): overview, evaluation, opportunities and challenges (2021)

11. Wu, J., Liu, J., Zhao, Y., Zheng, Z.: Analysis of cryptocurrency transactions from a network perspective: an overview. J. Netw. Comput. Appl. **190**, 103139 (2021). https://doi.org/10.1016/j.jnca.2021.103139, https://www.sciencedirect.com/science/article/pii/S1084804521001557

12. Yang, Z., et al.: Understanding retweeting behaviors in social networks. In: Proceedings of the 19th ACM International Conference on Information and Knowledge Management, CIKM '10, pp. 1633–1636. Association for Computing Machinery, New York (2010). https://doi.org/10.1145/1871437.1871691

13. Zhao, L., Sen Gupta, S., Khan, A., Luo, R.: Temporal analysis of the entire Ethereum blockchain network. In: Proceedings of the Web Conference 2021, WWW '21, pp. 2258–2269. Association for Computing Machinery, New York (2021). https://doi.org/10.1145/3442381.3449916

The Benefits of Non-Fungible Token (NFT) Technology in Music Copyright

Jie Dong[✉], Naipeng Dong, and Guangdong Bai

The University of Queensland, St Lucia, QLD, Australia
{uqjdong1,n.dong,g.bai}@uq.edu.au

Abstract. The emergence of Non-Fungible Tokens (NFTs) has presented a novel opportunity to address long-standing challenges in the realm of music copyright. This research paper explores the current iterations of NFTs as a potential solution for music copyright in the digital age. By leveraging blockchain technology, NFTs offer a unique and secure method for establishing ownership, verifying authenticity, and enabling direct artist compensation. This study examines the application of NFTs in the music industry, highlighting their potential impact on copyright management, royalty distribution, fan engagement, and licensing processes. Furthermore, the paper discusses the implications and limitations of adopting NFTs as a copyright solution and addresses potential legal and regulatory considerations. By shedding light on the intersection of NFTs and music copyright, this research aims to contribute to the ongoing discourse surrounding the transformative potential of blockchain technology in the music industry and its implications for creators, copyright holders, and music enthusiasts alike.

1 Introduction

In today's digital landscape, the protection of intellectual property, particularly in the realm of creative works such as music, has become increasingly challenging. Traditional copyright systems often struggle to address the complexities and nuances of the digital age, leading to issues of piracy, unauthorised usage, and inadequate compensation for artists and copyright holders [8]. However, the emergence of Non-Fungible Tokens (NFTs) presents a potential avenue for transforming copyright management and addressing these challenges. While initially popularised in the art world, NFTs have gained traction across various industries, including music [11].

The aim of this research paper is to explore the benefits of NFT technology in copyright management, with a specific focus on the music industry. By examining the potential advantages offered by NFTs, we seek to shed light on how this technology can revolutionise copyright practices. Additionally, this paper aims to identify potential challenges and considerations that accompany the implementation of NFT-based copyright systems.

In this study, we undertook a comprehensive analysis of the existing challenges within the music copyright domain. Subsequently, a solution harnessing NFT and blockchain technologies was proposed to address these issues.

N. Dong et al. (Eds.): SDLT 2023, CCIS 1975, pp. 98–105, 2024.
https://doi.org/10.1007/978-981-97-0006-6_7

2   Blockchain Technology and Its Role in NFTs

Blockchain Technology. Blockchain is a decentralised and distributed ledger system that facilitates secure and transparent recording of transactions across a network of computers (nodes). Consensus mechanisms, such as Proof of Work (PoW) or Proof of Stake (PoS), ensure data integrity and consensus among network participants. Role of Blockchain in NFTs are listed as follows:

Ownership and Provenance: Blockchain provides a transparent and trustworthy record of NFT ownership and transaction history, facilitating verification of ownership and establishing the provenance of digital assets [13].

Security and Immutability: NFTs leverage the cryptographic security and immutability inherent in blockchain, safeguarding these assets against tampering, duplication, or unauthorised modifications.

Decentralisation: Blockchain's decentralised nature ensures that NFTs are not controlled by any central authority, empowering peer-to-peer ownership, trading, and interactions within the ecosystem [7].

Smart Contracts: NFTs often employ smart contracts, programmable contracts executed on the blockchain, to define and enforce rules and functionalities. Smart contracts enable the automation of various processes related to NFTs, such as royalty distributions, licensing agreements, or access control mechanisms.

3   Related Works

This section introduces studies and solutions from academic and industry foundations.

The project in discussion presents a novel web-based music marketplace that incorporates digital watermarking technology to address these challenges. Central to this platform's copyright protection mechanism is the process of embedding a buyer-specific digital watermark into music files upon purchase. This watermarking approach ensures that every distributed music file carries a unique, encrypted identifier corresponding to its buyer. [14]

This next study examines the potential of repurposing Shazam's algorithm within a web application framework to address copyright concerns.

In the described project, as new music files are uploaded to the web application, they undergo analysis using Shazam's audio fingerprinting mechanism. The underlying process involves creating a distinct 'fingerprint' for the uploaded audio sample. Subsequently, this fingerprint is checked against Shazam's existing database for potential matches. If the system identifies a corresponding audio sample within its database, it indicates a possible breach of copyright regulations, as the uploaded track is not unique. [9]

JAAK is a technology company that aims to revolutionize the media and entertainment industry through blockchain-based solutions. The company's primary focus is on creating a decentralized infrastructure to streamline rights management, licensing, and royalty payments for digital content creators, distributors, and consumers. [1]

Ujo Music is a blockchain-based platform that aims to empower musicians and artists by providing them with more control over their creative works, revenue streams, and rights management. Developed on the Ethereum blockchain, Ujo Music offers a decentralized ecosystem that leverages smart contracts to streamline music distribution, licensing, and royalty payments. [2]

Lifehash is a company that provides blockchain solutions for various industries, such as insurance, supply chain, and personal data security. One of Lifehash's focus is tackling proof of ownership for copyright and IP, and they do this by storing content on the blockchain. [3]

4   Copyright Challenges and Traditional Approaches

4.1   Proving Ownership

Artists and labels have consistently faced the challenge of proving ownership of their musical creations [10]. Establishing a clear record of ownership is crucial in defending against copyright infringements [12].

Traditional Approach: To establish a public record of their copyright, artists and labels typically register their work with national copyright offices. Another method, known as the "poor man's copyright," involves mailing oneself a copy of the work to have a date-stamped proof, though its legal standing can be questionable. In Australia, it is not a requirement for artists to formally register their work to receive copyright protection, but it is in artists best interests to have a way to show proof of originality. [4]

4.2   Licensing Complexity

Licensing copyrighted works can be complex, time-consuming, and involve multiple rights holders, leading to difficulties in obtaining permissions and hindering lawful use [6]. In general, there are six types of music licences, each granting a different set of permissions. In the absence of a licensing organisation, users wanting to obtain a licence will need to negotiate with the artist directly. [5]

Traditional Approaches: Collective management organisations (CMOs) have been established to simplify the licensing process by acting as intermediaries between copyright holders and users. They negotiate and administer licences, collect and distribute royalties, and provide a centralised platform for licensing transactions. Standardised licensing agreements and digital licensing platforms have also been developed to streamline licensing processes. However, if you require multiple licences, they may need to be obtained through different organisations.

4.3   Royalty Tracking and Copyright Fractionalised Ownership

Ensuring accurate tracking of music usage and the consequent distribution of royalties has always been a nuanced challenge, further complicated by the collaborative nature of music creation. Multiple parties often have stakes in a single piece, leading to fragmented ownership, which makes rights management, tracking, and revenue distribution intricate.

Traditional Approaches: Performance rights organisations (PROs) and intermediaries have been the backbone of monitoring music plays across various platforms and venues. They collect and distribute the resulting royalties. Alongside this, licensing agencies and publishers have traditionally managed the complex web of rights, ensuring that each stakeholder's contributions and rights are appropriately accounted for, and revenues are distributed accordingly.

5   Proposed Solution: Integrating NFTs into Music Copyright and Licensing Management

We propose a decentralised, web-based marketplace employing blockchain technology to integrate non-fungible tokens (NFTs) as a mechanism for managing music copyrights and licences (Fig. 1).

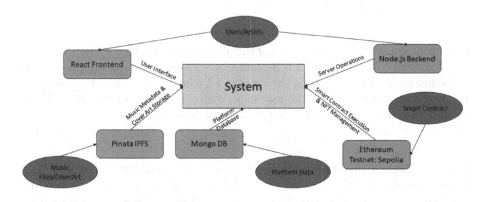

Fig. 1. System Overview

5.1   Music Tokenization Through NFTs

Upon uploading, each musical piece is tokenized, resulting in the creation of a unique NFT stored on the blockchain, which acts as a digital certificate of authenticity and ownership. The implications of this mechanism are multifaceted: it ensures a transparent, auditable history for each music piece, fortifies security through decentralised ledgers that mitigate unauthorised tampering or counterfeiting, and introduces novel avenues for artists to monetise their intellectual property.

5.2 Licensing Framework Integrated with NFTs

Instead of an outright transfer of full copyright, artists can opt to issue licences. These licences are conceptualised and represented as unique NFTs, each imbued with metadata specifying the scope of usage rights, duration, and other relevant terms. Users can choose from an array of licences made available by the artist that best suit their needs. This integrated approach redefines the licensing landscape. It enables unparalleled versatility by accommodating multiple concurrent licences for a singular music piece, catering to varied use-cases. Further, it assures all stakeholders of the authenticity of licensing agreements via an immutable blockchain record. Finally, the incorporation of smart contracts automates the royalty disbursement process in real-time, based on the stipulations of the licensing agreements.

6 Design Overview: Prototype Implementation

The prototype intricately integrates various technologies to achieve a blend of functionality and scalability. This section introduces the design and integration of these technologies within the system.

Frontend: React. The user interface of the marketplace is driven by React, a popular JavaScript library. React's component-based architecture ensures a uniform and efficient design by enabling the reuse of UI components across the platform. Its reactive nature enhances the user experience, providing immediate feedback by updating the UI in real-time based on data changes.

Backend: Node.js. Serving as the backbone of backend operations is Node.js, a JavaScript runtime environment. Its asynchronous nature is ideal for managing multiple concurrent user requests, ensuring rapid and efficient server responses. Coupled with the vast library of packages available through the Node Package Manager (NPM), the system achieves both functionality and rapid development.

Storage: Pinata IPFS and MongoDB. For the storage of metadata associated with music files and cover art, the prototype utilises the InterPlanetary File System (IPFS) via Pinata, a cloud service specialising in IPFS pinning. Complementing IPFS, MongoDB, a NoSQL database, handles platform-related data storage including price and for sale status. Having these components managed by an external database is much more cost efficient than writing and storing on the blockchain.

Smart Contracts: Solidity on Ethereum Testnet. Smart contracts form the crux of the marketplace's operations. Authored in Solidity, these contracts are deployed on the Ethereum Testnet, offering transparency through the blockchain's open ledger. The smart contract handles core functionality such as NFT minting and transfer of ownership.

System Interaction Flow. The interaction begins with users interfacing with the React-based UI, triggering various requests. These are managed by Node.js, which interfaces with the Ethereum Testnet or the appropriate databases. The user can choose to login with their digital wallet, or remain disconnected and continue to browse the marketplace. Choosing to login allows the user to perform tasks such as minting and purchasing. Upon logging in, a blanket profile is created on MongoDB centred on the users wallet address. Users will have the option to customise their profile. On the next page you can find Fig. 2, a User flow diagram for artists and buyers.

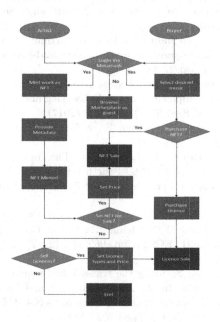

Fig. 2. User flow Diagram

Depending on the data type, the backend either communicates with Pinata IPFS or MongoDB. For instance, while music metadata is sourced from IPFS, user account details are fetched from MongoDB. For operations central to minting NFTs or purchasing licences, the system interacts with smart contracts on the Ethereum Testnet.

7 Conclusion

Non-fungible tokens (NFTs) have been posited as a novel approach to address various challenges in the digital copyright domain. The primary attribute of NFTs is their ability to provide unique, immutable representation for digital assets on a decentralised ledger. This can facilitate transparent tracking and potentially simplify the intricacies associated with establishing digital ownership. The inherent qualities of blockchain, the underlying technology, offer the possibility for more precise copyright management in the digital realm, aiming to reduce rights ambiguity. Our solution provides an alternative to copyright protection and license management, by addressing challenges such as licensing complexity and proving ownership.

References

1. https://www.crunchbase.com/organization/jaak. Accessed 25 July 2023
2. https://www.gemtracks.com/guides/view.php?title=ujo-music-review&id=1921. Accessed 25 July 2023
3. https://www.lifehash.com/industries/ip-and-copyright. Accessed 27 July 2023
4. https://www.lifehash.com/post/prove-ownership-and-protect-your-copyright-with-blockchain. Accessed 27 July 2023
5. https://www.apraamcos.com.au/. Accessed 15 July 2023
6. Whorton, A.M.: The complexities of music licensing and the need for revised legal regime. Wake For. Law Rev. **52**(1), 267–292 (2017)
7. Narayanan, A., Bonneau, J., Felten, E., Miller, A., Goldfeder, S.: Bitcoin and Cryptocurrency Technologies
8. Campidoglio, M., Frattolillo, F., Landolfi, F.: The copyright protection problem: challenges and suggestions. In: 2009 Fourth International Conference on Internet and Web Applications and Services, pp. 522–526 (2009). https://doi.org/10.1109/ICIW.2009.84
9. Jiang, Y., Zhou, J.: Digital music copyright protection system based on blockchain. In: 2022 4th International Academic Exchange Conference on Science and Technology Innovation (IAECST), pp. 962–966 (2022). https://doi.org/10.1109/IAECST57965.2022.10062214
10. Kaushik, A., Malik, M.: Securing the transfer and controlling the piracy of digital files using blockchain. In: 2022 Fifth International Conference on Computational Intelligence and Communication Technologies (CCICT), pp. 324–331 (2022). https://doi.org/10.1109/CCiCT56684.2022.00066
11. Roth, E.: https://www.theverge.com/2022/5/16/23074909/spotify-experiments-musician-nft-galleries. Accessed 19 July 2023
12. Tan, L.: https://legalvision.com.au/sinking-ship-federal-court-orders-isps-to-block-pirate-sites-in-australia/. Accessed 26 July 2023

13. Tharun, T., Vamshi, A., Eswari, R.: NFT application for music industry using blockchain smart contracts. In: 2023 4th International Conference on Innovative Trends in Information Technology (ICITIIT), pp. 1–6 (2023). https://doi.org/10.1109/ICITIIT57246.2023.10068684

14. Zhao, S., O'Mahony, D.: BMCProtector: a blockchain and smart contract based application for music copyright protection. In: Proceedings of the 2018 International Conference on Blockchain Technology and Application, ICBTA '18, pp 1–5. Association for Computing Machinery, New York (2018). https://doi.org/10.1145/3301403.3301404

Central Bank Digital Currency Models
A Short Review

Hei Lam Yip and Babu Pillai[✉]

Faculty of Science and Engineering, Southern Cross University, Gold Coast, Australia
kittyicq@hotmail.com, pillai.babu@outlook.com

Abstract. This research paper explores the models and implications of central bank digital currency (CBDC) in four countries: China, Japan, the U.S., and Australia. The paper analyses the different design choices, governance structures, and technological challenges of CBDC development in each country. The paper also compares the progress and impact of CBDC on financial stability, privacy, and centralised control. The paper concludes that CBDCs have the potential to revolutionise digital payment systems and enhance the efficiency and security of transactions, but they also pose significant risks and trade-offs that need to be carefully addressed. The paper provides some recommendations for CBDC development and adoption, such as establishing comprehensive regulations, educating the public, and ensuring interoperability.

Keywords: CBDC · digital currency · cryptocurrency · blockchain · DLT

1 Introduction

Over the past two decades, groundbreaking technologies have revolutionised monetary and payment systems at an unparalleled rate. The advent of various digital currencies—ranging from mobile money to cryptocurrencies underpinned by distributed ledger technology and blockchain—has consistently tested the limits of existing domestic and international financial regulations. Moreover, the surge of unregulated crypto-digital currencies has unleashed a wave of fraud, theft, and hacking incidents, jeopardising the established financial frameworks overseen by national regulatory bodies such as central banks. To counter these challenges, especially those tied to the anonymity of traditional digital currencies, central banks across the globe are actively investigating the viability of launching state-sanctioned, centrally-backed digital currencies.

As Central Bank Digital Currency (CBDC) remains under active research and development, a standardised, conclusive definition is yet to exist [19]. However, it generally possesses three distinctive characteristics that set it apart from physical cash, electronic money, and traditional cryptocurrencies [8]. First, CBDC is issued by a central bank, representing a liability of that institution rather than a private financial entity, and it is expected to hold a value analogous to the fiat currency distributed by the same central bank. Second, CBDC is

N. Dong et al. (Eds.): SDLT 2023, CCIS 1975, pp. 106–123, 2024.
https://doi.org/10.1007/978-981-97-0006-6_8

virtual, existing solely in digital form as opposed to a physical medium. Third, although CBDC may employ technologies like blockchain or distributed ledger technology for transaction and settlement processes, it remains under the centralised control and supervision of the issuing central bank.

Worldwide, various banking analyst reports and academic studies have delved into the pros and cons of CBDC [29]. On the upside, CBDCs offer advantages such as efficiency, convenience, safety, integrity, accessibility, settlement finality, and financial inclusion. Conversely, the risks often centre around the potential misuse of financial data and concerns regarding user privacy. Despite the evolving dialogue and research focusing on the financial and technological aspects of CBDC, there is a notable gap in legal and policy analysis concerning the regulation of information protection associated with CBDC.

The insights garnered from this paper will hold far-reaching implications for state-sponsored digital currencies in various jurisdictions. Particularly, when the advent of CBDCs introduces potential or significant risks to financial markets and individual privacy, a legal framework becomes imperative to confront these challenges and to offer viable solutions. Prior to delving into the practical and regulatory complexities of CBDCs, an essential preliminary step involves examining the available design options, as these choices will invariably influence the future regulatory landscape for CBDCs.

The main contributions of this paper are:

- Analyses CBDC models for four countries: China, Japan, the U.S., and Australia.
- Compares the CBDC progress, highlighting the factors that influence their development and adoption.
- Provides some recommendations for CBDC development and adoption.

2   Background

A large number of recent studies examine the dynamics of digital currency cryptocurrencies, CBDC and potential impact central banking monetary policy. policies [10, 14, 22]. This section give a brief background into digital payment, CBDC its design.

2.1   Digital Payment Systems

Digital payments, often referred to as electronic payment systems, involve the transfer of digital money between accounts through the use of digital payment technologies. These technologies encompass a wide range of methods to facilitate electronic transfers of funds. Advancements in technology, combined with increased access to digital devices and internet connectivity, have spurred the transformation toward digital payments.

In our conventional financial architecture, when central banks allocate credit to commercial banks, this allocation gets registered in the ledgers of these commercial banks as a credit from the central bank. This credit is not relayed directly to the individual bank customers. Instead, commercial banks draw upon this credit to disburse retail money to their clientele in the form of digital transactions and deposits. The digital funds reflected in the accounts of customers denote adjustments in their account balances and don't represent tangible cash. Conversely, tangible currency is the sole monetary format provided by central banks that consumers can directly possess and transact with.

The shift toward digital, cashless payments offers a plethora of advantages for consumers, enterprises, and governments alike. Not only are these payments swift, secure, and convenient, but they also diminish the overheads associated with cash management for banks and financial institutions. Both government bodies and financial institutions have been instrumental in championing the transition to digital cashless payment infrastructures.

Digital currency offers the dual advantages of rapid access to funds and unparalleled convenience for users. Furthermore, it provides governmental agencies and tax authorities with enhanced capabilities for tracking the flow of money, thereby aiding in the detection of tax evasion and money laundering activities.

2.2   CBDCs

CBDCs are digital currencies that are issued and overseen by a central bank. An immediate inquiry surfaces: With the prevailing money system predominantly digital, what differentiates a CBDC?. While a digital currency signifies a claim against an intermediary, a CBDC embodies a direct claim against the central bank [4]. This is in contrast to cryptocurrencies, which are shaped, transacted, and terminated via open protocols. In the case of CBDCs, their issuance and governance rest with the central bank, mirroring the operations of conventional fiat currency. Several central banks, in their exploration of CBDCs, emphasise the potential of these currencies to amplify financial inclusion, as highlighted in a report [17] by the Bank for International Settlements (BIS)[1].

In essence, a CBDC is conceived as a digital counterpart aiming to emulate the foundational functions of physical currency [29]. It aspires to ensure universal access, function as legal tender, and its provenance can be easily traced. A CBDC is structured to fulfill quintessential monetary functions, serving as a unit of account, a medium for exchange, and a reservoir for value.

The discourse around CBDCs often gravitates towards their potential to act as digital cash, encapsulating features that support peer-to-peer transactions and operations without the need for online connectivity. The objective is to digitally encapsulate the attributes of tangible cash, ensuring it is amenable for regular transactions and remains accessible, even in the absence of internet connectivity. However, the exact design and operational nuances of CBDCs can diverge, contingent on the stipulations and choices of the individual central banks.

---

[1] https://www.bis.org/about/bisih/topics/cbdc.htm.

Conceiving CBDCs as digital equivalents to physical cash, such as tendering a banknote or coin [6]. A meticulously crafted CBDC is not just a digital facsimile of a nation's currency; it has the potential to serve multifarious policy aims. The design of CBDCs is not to replace but to coexist alongside tangible currency, offering an alternative underpinned by the merits of digital evolution. While retaining many attributes of traditional tender, like stability and universal acceptance within its territory, CBDCs can proffer benefits like streamlined transactions, cost-effectiveness, and fortified security provisions.

2.3   Navigating the Emergence of CBDCs

For centuries, people have relied on paper currency, making the shift to digital currency a challenging transition, especially for older generations. The currency system is fundamentally built on trust, and if the public lacks confidence in CBDC, it remains merely a string of meaningless digits. The question then arises: what underpins this new technology? Is it the central banks, the government, or perhaps mathematical algorithms? Trust is the bedrock, but skepticism exists about whether machines can establish this trust. Additionally, the regulatory framework for CBDCs is still in its infancy, lacking comprehensive laws to protect digital assets. Even governmental authorities are uncertain about the repercussions of CBDC issuance. On a practical note, widespread acceptance is also hampered by the lack of merchant facilities that accept CBDCs, akin to promoting electric vehicles without providing enough charging stations.

CBDCs are experiencing a surge in popularity globally, emerging as a prominent digital payment system. An increasing number of people are opting to use digital payment methods to enhance the convenience of transactions. According to Jones [7], the objective of a CBDC is to serve as 'a digital claim on the central bank, accessible to the wider public.' As trust between the public and central banks solidifies, CBDCs have the potential to revolutionise our economy. Moreover, they could address numerous challenges in the current global economic system and offer improved control over inflation rates.

According to Náñez Alonso [21], 'CBDC is an electronic variant of cash issued by a central bank, which combines cryptography and digital ledger technology to offer this digital money.' This statement aptly encapsulates the ideal vision for central digital currency. Nonetheless, several challenges must be addressed before the full realisation of the CBDC system can occur. One primary issue is the integration of new technologies; there exists a segment of the population that does not yet utilise smartphones or any digital devices. Transitioning from a reliance on physical assets to adopting digital assets is not straightforward; altering people's mindsets and fostering trust in the new system is a time-intensive process. As Peterson notes [24], individual choice will play a crucial role in the acceptance of new digital currency despite the remarkable technology it employs. Another significant hurdle is the current inadequacy of regulations and infrastructure surrounding digital currency [11]; this can potentially allow individuals to exploit the system, thereby creating risks for the general public. The existing support for CBDCs is insufficient, posing threats to financial stability. Furthermore, digitally illiterate individuals may require assistance from physical human agents, necessitating direct communication with a real person to address their queries [24].

2.4   CBDC Design

There are two prominent types of CBDC designs being developed. The first is based on DLT, and the second operates under central control [9].

DLT-based CBDCs draw upon the concept of decentralised cryptocurrencies, addressing the illegitimacy issues associated with complete anonymity by incorporating validation by authorised verifiers. DLT-related design currencies stand distinct from electronic currencies based on a trusted central payment system. Compared to a centralised intermediary payment system, the DLT design of CBDCs could facilitate business transactions and financial services due to its accessibility, resilience, and transparency. However, a CBDC with a DLT design is not without risks. The evolving DLTs may bring operational and security risks and potential disruptions to the current monetary regulation. For instance, the multiple nodes of a DLT can create additional entry points for malicious intruders, cryptographic tools might experience security breaches, and existing regulations may not be robust enough to confirm the rights and obligations of involved parties. Additionally, non-central bank parties involved in a DLT-based CBDC might partake in various CBDC transactions without sufficient security measures, akin to a country's central bank, leading to additional financial risks.

A centralised model of CBDC design, where the central bank has exclusive control over the digital currency, poses several concerns that warrant careful consideration. One glaring issue is that this model may raise serious privacy concerns, as the central entity monitors and records all transactions, possibly compromising the confidentiality of users' financial activities. Moreover, innovation may be stifled due to a lack of competitive atmosphere encouraging the development of new features and improvements. The centralised structure might also breed bureaucratic inefficiencies, slowing down necessary adaptations to evolving market conditions and possibly leading to mismanagement or abuse of authority. Thus, a well-thought-out approach addressing aspects like security, privacy, and scalability is imperative when contemplating a centralised CBDC design.

3   CBDC Models

3.1   China

According to Wang [28], the e-CNY, also known as the digital yuan — China's CBDC, is poised to be a formidable player both on the domestic and global stage, bolstered significantly by substantial backing from the Chinese government, akin to its fiat currency. The e-CNY operates on a two-tier system, supplemented with auxiliary layers to facilitate service delivery to end-users. This digital currency is characterised by features like proficient circulation management, seamless interoperability, and a flexible exchange and wallet ecosystem. Remarkably, these features are accessible to both Chinese residents and foreign visitors in China [28] (Fig. 1).

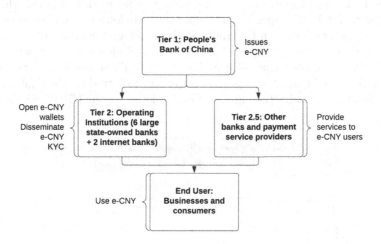

Fig. 1. The e-CNY structure [5].

The structure of e-CNY is centralised, under the central government's stringent oversight. At the core of this structure is the People's Bank of China (PBOC), which occupies the first tier, responsible for dispensing e-CNY to the second-tier entities. These second-tier institutions comprise six prominent state-owned banks and two leading internet banks in China, tasked with the role of initiating e-CNY wallets or accounts for the general populace. The state-owned banks enlisted in this endeavour are the Bank of China (BOC), China Construction Bank (CCB), Industrial and Commercial Bank of China (ICBC), Agricultural Bank of China (ABC), Bank of Communications (BOCOM), and the Postal Savings Bank of China (PSBC), complemented by the internet banking giants, WeBank (associated with Weixin Pay) and MYbank (affiliated with Alipay) [30]. These institutions function as conduits, channelling the service down to other commercial banks, enterprises, consumers, and payment service providers, thereby facilitating a seamless flow of transactions within the ecosystem. To illustrate, individuals can readily convert conventional CNY to e-CNY or digital yuan via these state banks. The converted currency can then be safely stored in an e-CNY wallet, empowering users to execute transactions or procure goods from providers integrated with the e-CNY network.

3.2 Japan

The Bank of Japan, as the nation's central bank, is responsible for issuing the Yen, Japan's fiat currency, to the public. It is also likely to be the institution behind the issuance of Japan's CBDC, commonly referred to as the digital yen. The Bank of Japan has already taken several significant steps towards this end. It published a CBDC paper in November 2020, followed by the release of the Proof of Concept Phase 1 in December 2021 and Phase 2 in May 2022[2]. Further, it has scheduled a Pilot Program for May 2023 and aims for an official issuance by February 2026, according to available data [1]. These developments indicate that the Bank of Japan is on a phased trajectory to introduce the digital yen by 2026, following extensive testing and public piloting of the CBDC scheme.

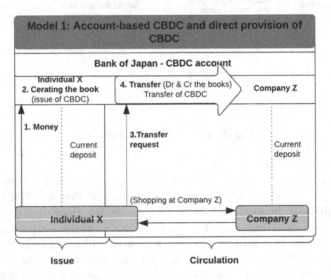

Fig. 2. Model 1 – Account-based CBDC with direct provision [13]

Masayoshi Amamiya, the Deputy Governor of the Bank of Japan, has outlined two primary forms of CBDC. The first is an *account-based CBDC*, where individuals and firms open accounts directly with the central bank and utilise these for transfers. The second form is a *token-based CBDC*, which involves users storing CBDC on smartphone applications or IC cards and transferring value for payments [2]. Figure 2 and Fig. 3 provide further details on these account-based CBDC structures, categorised into direct and indirect provisions. In the direct account model, an individual—referred to as X can transfer CBDC directly from their own digital wallet or account to a Company Z. Conversely, the indirect account model involves an Intermediating Institution Y. In this model, individual X first transfers yen to Institution Y, which then converts it into digital yen.

---

[2] https://www.boj.or.jp/en/paym/digital/index.htm.

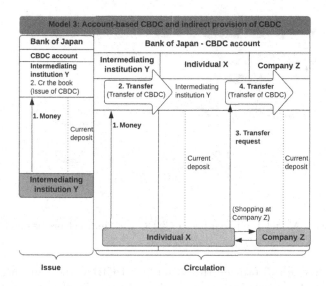

Fig. 3. Model 3 – Account-based CBDC with indirect provision [13]

Subsequently, individual X can transfer this digital yen to Company Z. In this scenario, Institution Y serves as a currency exchange entity, adding an extra layer of conversion from yen to digital yen.

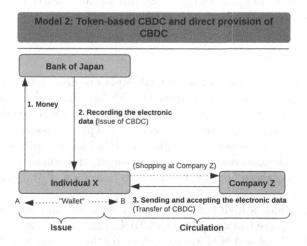

Fig. 4. Model 2 – Token-based CBDC with direct provision [13]

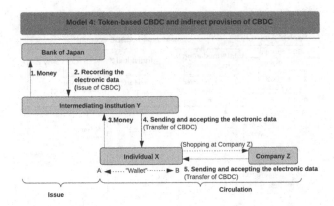

Fig. 5. Model 4 – Token-based CBDC with indirect provision [13]

Figure 4 and Fig. 5 provide the token-based CBDC mechanisms, differentiating between direct and indirect provisions. In the direct token method, users can transfer CBDC using either their ID card or smartphone. Upon receiving the electronic token data from the user's ID card or smartphone, the Bank of Japan can validate the transaction and initiate the CBDC transfer to Company Z. The indirect token method operates similarly, but includes an additional layer: Intermediating Institution Y. This entity decrypts the electronic data before forwarding it to the Bank of Japan. Once the Bank of Japan receives and approves this data, Intermediating Institution Y is authorised to proceed with the CBDC transfer to Company Z.

3.3   United States

In 2022, the Biden administration set forth a plan to delve into CBDCs, aiming to mitigate fraud and enhance security [15]. Federal Reserve Chair, Jerome H. Powell, emphasised that the creation of a CBDC involves addressing monetary policy, financial stability, consumer protection, and privacy issues [12]. The intention is clear: the U.S. wants to introduce a CBDC for its citizens, but it must first address public concerns, regulatory challenges, and potential data breaches. Without resolving these hurdles, the path to launching digital dollars remains uncertain.

Figure 6 provides a high-level view of the approval and issuance of CBDC tokens. Before reserve banks can issue a CBDC, the proposal would first need to be approved by the Board of Governors. It would then be submitted to Congress for further review. Congress would then debate the merits and potential drawbacks of the initiative before deciding if reserve banks can proceed with issuing the CBDC to the public. Once approved, the CBDC would go through the process of being issued to commercial banks, service providers, and ultimately, to customers. It is important to highlight that states may differ in their perspectives or timelines concerning the CBDC. Thereafter, consumers can opt for

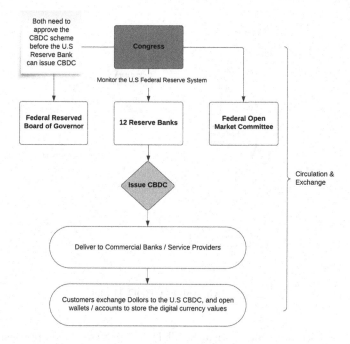

Fig. 6. U.S. CBDC Model

digital wallets via these banks, facilitating the conversion of physical dollars into their digital counterparts.

3.4   Australia

The Reserve Bank of Australia (RBA) is cooperating with the Digital Finance Cooperative Research Centre (DFCRC) to investigate the economic benefits that CBDC can bring to Australia; a few projects outlining the use cases, benefits and limitations of Australia CBDC have become popular among the researchers [27].

Australia, in particular, is at an interesting juncture in the CBDC landscape. The nation has primarily been focusing on the research and exploratory phase, delving deep into understanding the implications, benefits, and challenges of launching its own CBDC. Recognising the profound impact such a currency can have on its economy and society at large, Australian policymakers believe that it's crucial to involve the broader community in this conversation. There is a pressing need for more public discussions, seminars, and speeches to not only educate the masses about CBDCs but also to gauge their perspective and draw their attention to the potential transformation in the financial realm.

As depicted in Fig. 7, an overview of the Australian CBDC model is presented. At the core of this model, the central banks play a pivotal role by issuing CBDCs to commercial banks. These commercial banks, having vast experience and infrastructure in handling retail financial services, are then responsible for all

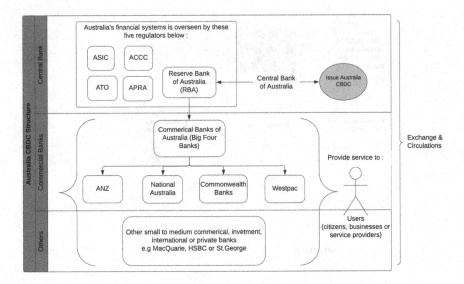

Fig. 7. Australian CBDC Model

user-facing services associated with the CBDC. This two-tiered approach ensures that while the integrity and authenticity of the digital currency are maintained by the central authority, the distribution, and transactional services are managed by institutions that are closely integrated with the end-users.

3.5 Discussions

Due to its centralised governance model, China has the capacity to promote its CBDC, known as e-CNY, on a broad scale. This enables an extensive scope for trials and experiments, facilitating data collection that could inform improvements to the existing financial system. Notably, significant resources have been allocated for CBDC research and pilot programs, signalling a strong intent to bring e-CNY into mainstream usage in the near future. While public opinion on the stability and acceptance of CBDCs may vary, the government's commitment to its implementation suggests that any reservations will likely be carefully considered as part of its ongoing development strategy.

In the context of a decentralised financial system, Japan's approach to CBDC development appears to involve multiple layers of governance, including both central and local authorities. The Bank of Japan has set timelines, with a goal of introducing a digital yen by 2026. Public consultation and expert input are being sought to inform the selection of the most beneficial CBDC model for the country. Various options are presented for stakeholder consideration, and local governments can share their viewpoints with the central authority. This collaborative and consultative approach may contribute to a more thorough preparatory phase, potentially mitigating challenges that could arise during later implementation stages.

In the United States, the financial system and cultural attitudes toward finance add layers of complexity to the development and adoption of a CBDC. Public concerns around data privacy are notable, and no absolute guarantee of data security exists. Moreover, the governance structure in the U.S. is decentralised, with varying relationships between the central and state governments. This could present challenges in reaching a consensus among diverse parties with differing interests, especially when it comes to advancing CBDC initiatives.

In Australia, the governance system is also decentralised, allowing state governments considerable autonomy in certain regulatory matters. As a result, more developed states might be quicker to experiment with CBDCs, while more remote states could lag in adoption. Although public discourse on digital currencies has been relatively limited, likely due to media focus on cryptocurrencies, increasing research and public discussion are anticipated to elevate awareness. While there may be some resistance to adopting new financial technologies, given Australia's generally cautious approach to change, the long-term benefits to the financial system could prompt earlier trials and eventual adoption of a CBDC.

In a centralised governance structure, the development and deployment of a CBDC may progress more quickly. This is because decision-making could be more streamlined and efficient. On the other hand, a decentralised governance approach might lead to a more robust and well-considered digital currency in the long term. While strong government support could be an asset during the initial stages of launching a digital currency, the ultimate success of the currency depends on its long-term impact on the economy and its acceptance by the public. If the digital currency proves beneficial, it will likely gain widespread acceptance. However, if it proves to be detrimental, there may be negative repercussions, potentially undermining public trust and adoption.

4 Observations on CBDC Dynamics

For the widespread adoption of CBDC, comprehensive regulations are essential to ensure the rights and protections of digital currency users. Without safeguarding digital assets under legal frameworks, it becomes challenging to encourage the public to embrace this new form of currency. For instance, the existence of fraudulent cryptocurrency platforms raises concerns about reliability [8]. Similarly, without governing regulations for CBDCs, it is difficult to control the spread of misinformation or establish authoritative assessments of various digital currencies. Additionally, the government should actively promote the deployment of authorised payment terminals that support CBDC transactions, thereby expanding the number of outlets where customers can use digital currency.

Addressing and changing public perceptions about CBDC is crucial for its successful implementation. Government bodies have a role to play in educating the public on what this new technology means for society. Training sessions and complimentary CBDC cards for trial use could help familiarise people with the system. Misinformation is another challenge; some media outlets have misconstrued the essence of CBDC, sowing confusion and scepticism among the public.

Failure to correct these misconceptions can lead to increased doubt and hesitancy to adopt this groundbreaking technology. Therefore, engaging in educational initiatives that inform the public about the real objectives, features, and long-term benefits of CBDCs for the economy.

In the following sections, we explore the multifaceted nature of CBDCs, touching upon technological advancements, financial stability implications, privacy considerations, and the intricacies of centralised oversight.

4.1   Technological Advancement

In an era characterised by swift technological innovations, the financial services landscape is undergoing transformative changes, with central banks at the forefront of this evolution. Recognising the pivotal role of technology in shaping consumer expectations, central banks globally are keen on integrating these advancements into their operational transition strategies from physical to digital money. Esteemed institutions, from the People's Bank of China (PBOC) to the Reserve Bank of Australia (RBA) and the US Federal Reserve, are now actively exploring or implementing CBDCs, marking a significant milestone in the realm of digital finance. Several compelling drivers underscore this interest: the global shift away from cash, especially magnified during the pandemic; the rising prominence of private digital assets; the opportunity for central banks to reestablish themselves as pioneers in financial innovation; and the aspiration to exert granular control over globalised payment systems for regional stability.

Diving deeper into national trajectories, China's financial landscape, already revolutionised by platforms like Alipay and WeChat, is poised for further evolution with the anticipated rollout of the digital yuan. Japan has been increasingly warming up to mobile payments since the Tokyo 2020 Olympics, signifying this shift and hinting at the potential of a digital Yen in the future. In the U.S., the ascent of digital wallets, such as *Apple Pay* and *Android Pay*, and the broadening embrace of digital payments indicate the ripe landscape for a possible U.S. CBDC. Meanwhile, Australia, already witnessing a surge in electronic transactions and innovations like the 2018 *New Payments Platform* [23,25], is exploring the nation's commitment to financial technological progress. In sum, the convergence of technology and finance is an observable trend and a strategic imperative for central banks worldwide.

4.2   Financial Stability

The rise of digital currencies, most notably led by Bitcoin [20] and further bolstered by the recognition of stablecoins, has urged central banks worldwide to contemplate the inception of their CBDCs. This move seeks to retain their significance and ensure they remain pivotal in the international monetary spectrum. An underlying concern for central banks is the potential undermining of their monetary policy influence if decentralised cryptocurrencies gain vast acceptance, which may lead to financial instability and fraud. Despite its historical dominance, physical paper currency is fraught with logistical challenges, primarily due to its need for physical transference between entities. CBDCs aim to eliminate such logistical burdens as they are account-based digital entities [16]. Traditional banks can sometimes be impeded from promptly furnishing funds to their clients during financial adversities. However, CBDCs, necessitating fewer secure assets, ensure the financial landscape remains robust, thus fostering stability [3]. Moreover, CBDCs, due to their inherent traceability, act as a defence against illicit financial undertakings, such as money laundering. This ensures that each transaction is scrutinised, enabling oversight bodies to discern and act upon any anomalous transactions that could threaten financial stability.

4.3 Privacy

Privacy is a paramount concern in the development of CBDC, with the central challenge being to balance individual privacy rights against the transparency mandates of anti-money laundering (AML) regulations. Privacy risks in current CBDC models can be distilled into four main categories: loss of regulatory control, loss of anonymity, loss of individual control, and loss of liberty [26]. As we delve deeper, we will examine how different countries, including China, Japan, the U.S.A., and Australia, address these privacy risks in their CBDC approaches.

In China, privacy is not considered a major concern by most citizens; instead, it is seen as a reality to be accepted. Given the centralised nature of China's economic and political systems, many of its citizens have faith in their government and are ready to prioritise the welfare of the majority over individual rights. Because of this political and cultural backdrop, Chinese citizens are likely to adapt to changes even if those entail some breaches of privacy. Fan Yifei, the Deputy Governor of the People's Bank of China, has remarked that while Central Bank Digital Currency (CBDC) transactions without third-party anonymity could jeopardise personal data and privacy, complete third-party anonymity might foster illicit activities, including tax evasion and terrorist financing [31]. A prevailing sentiment in China is that if an individual has not committed any wrongdoing, they should not be apprehensive about potential privacy intrusions or increased oversight, as they have nothing to hide. Conversely, these privacy issues are of significant concern to Western and other developed nations, placing pressure on the Chinese government to address the privacy aspects of the digital yuan on the global stage. To gain international trust, the Chinese government must vouch for the integrity of Chinese laws and assure foreigners that their privacy will be upheld within its legal framework. Achieving this will be demanding. If the Chinese government wishes to globalise the digital yuan, they must introduce more comprehensive privacy measures and demonstrate greater transparency in their policy decisions.

In Japan, the Bank of Japan is keen on striking a balance between preventing financial crimes and ensuring privacy in relation to the digital Yen. The bank has suggested incorporating advanced cryptography to ensure commercial banks cannot access information across different CBDC accounts, even if users hold multiple ones [18]. While the digital Yen is still in its developmental stages, many local citizens might be unaware of the intricacies behind the initiative. Nevertheless, prominent Japanese firms have partnered with the Japan CBDC pilot programs, pushing forward its development. These firms are vocal about user data management concerns and calling on the government for enhanced privacy measures. Given its status as the world's third-largest economy, there is significant international interest in Japan's CBDC rollout and the data protection technologies it will adopt.

In the US, the topic of privacy with respect to CBDC is a subject of intense debate. Many Americans question their government's ability to safeguard data protection adequately. The digital nature of CBDC records every transaction, amassing vast amounts of personal, financial, and locational data. Each digital dollar spent is tied to an individual, and a significant portion of the population is uneasy about the government tracking their purchases or even believing the government should not have the authority to do so. From the government's viewpoint, it might be seen as a necessary trade-off: while the CBDC enhances digital currency's capabilities, it might also mean individuals relinquishing some control over their data, similar to what is done with artificial intelligence, robotics, and automation. Amid the tension between the US government and its citizens, there is a pressing need for a thorough discourse to address and delineate the privacy implications, configurations, and protections surrounding CBDC.

In Australia, there is growing concern regarding how central banks handle user data. Many CBDC users anticipate a degree of anonymity for their transaction details. Individuals do not need to verify their identity with physical cash, but with CBDC, the situation is the opposite. Using Distributed Ledger Technology (DLT), the Australian government can track payment histories and geographical locations. If the relevant entities mishandle this sensitive data or inadvertently disclose it, the repercussions for society could be significant. This is a primary reason many Australians are calling for a robust privacy framework before the introduction of CBDC. While the e-AUD, or Australian CBDC, may not become a dominant global currency, its development will still draw attention. International businesses with ties to Australia will be keen to observe how the Australian government addresses privacy concerns associated with CBDC.

4.4   Centralised Control

Although decentralisation is a foundational characteristic of blockchain and was a primary feature of cryptocurrency's inception, central banks are leaning toward a centralised approach with the introduction of CBDCs.

In China, the Central Bank will exercise oversight over the CBDC, ensuring it can supervise, monitor, and trace its operations to mitigate financial crimes [31]. Unlike decentralized crypto assets, CBDCs are centralized, giving greater control to central banks and making them more secure and dependable digital payments. Central banks aim to maintain controlled anonymity to swiftly address illicit or unusual transactions. The introduction of CBDCs might diminish the population's interest in crypto assets, which are viewed as less secure by the Chinese government. This centralized approach to CBDC is intended to safeguard citizens' assets and fortify financial stability.

In Japan, a CBDC operates as electronic coins or accounts, fully backed by the government's credibility. Its ownership and denomination are tracked through a ledger that maintains a record of issuances and transactions. The Bank of Japan intends to maintain control over the CBDC, ensuring the technological viability of its three ledger designs: shared account-based, centralized token-based, and centralized account-based[3]. With its pilot program launched in April 2023, Japan aims for mainstream adoption of the digital currency to benefit local businesses by optimizing their payment systems. This centralized digital currency, endorsed by the Bank of Japan, fosters confidence among local enterprises and attracts international companies to support the digital Yen.

In the US, the allure of issuing a centralized digital currency to regain control over its decentralized financial system is significant. Many cryptocurrencies launched in the US lack robust financial backing, and some have misled countless investors with false promises. Unfortunately, current regulations offer limited oversight over these crypto assets and their issuers, leaving many investors vulnerable. Given the lack of transparency from some unregulated digital asset platforms, it becomes imperative for the US government to introduce its centralized digital currency, the CBDC, to safeguard its citizens' digital assets and exert more control over the digital financial landscape.

In Australia, the rollout of the CBDC is still pending due to challenges identified during the research phase. The private sector views the CBDC as not a replacement for digital payments but an adjunct[4]. While both the Australian government and the RBA recognise the benefits of introducing a CBDC, securing consensus within the nation's decentralised governance and financial systems is challenging. Centralised oversight of the CBDC could enable the RBA to better analyse interest rates, as digital currency backed by Distributed Ledger Technology (DLT) offers valuable transaction data, potentially leading to more accurate financial reporting than the current system allows. However, the formal acceptance of the CBDC in Australia might be a few years away, necessitating greater media emphasis on its significance.

5   Conclusion

This paper explores the models and implications of central bank digital currency (CBDC) in four countries: China, Japan, the U.S., and Australia. It analyses the different design choices, governance structures, and technological challenges of CBDC development in each country. It also compares the progress and impact of CBDC on financial stability, privacy, and centrality in control. The paper finds that CBDCs have the potential to revolutionise digital payment systems and enhance the efficiency and security of transactions but also pose significant risks

---

[3] https://www.lexology.com/library/detail.aspx?g=43ebd953-5327-4edc-9940-e193f7a6b04e.

[4] https://www.rba.gov.au/media-releases/2023/mr-23-21.html.

and trade-offs that need to be carefully addressed. The paper provides some recommendations for CBDC development and adoption, such as establishing comprehensive regulations, educating the public, and ensuring interoperability. The paper acknowledges the limitations of its scope and methodology and suggests further research on the legal, social, and economic aspects of CBDCs.

References

1. Alisha, C.: Snapshot: which countries have made the most progress on CBDCS so far in 2023. Econographics, Atlantic Councill (2019)
2. Amamiya, M.: Should the bank of japan issue a digital currency. In: Speech at a Reuters Newsmaker Event in Tokyo, Speech, Tokyo (5 July 2019)
3. Andolfatto, D.: Assessing the impact of central bank digital currency on private banks. Federal Reserve Bank of ST. Tech. Rep., Louis Working Paper 2018–026C (2018)
4. Auer, R., Böhme, R.: CBDC architectures, the financial system, and the central bank of the future. VoxEU. org-CEPR's Policy Portal (2020)
5. Bank, D.: Digital yuan: what is it and how does it work? (2021). https://www.db.com/news/detail/20210714-digital-yuan-what-is-it-and-how-does-it-work
6. Bindseil, U.: Tiered CBDC and the financial system. Available at SSRN 3513422 (2020)
7. Brad, J.: The economics of a central bank digital currency in Australia (2022). https://www.rba.gov.au/speeches/2022/sp-ag-2022-12-08.html
8. Carney, M.: The future of money. In: Scottish Economics Conference. Edinburgh University, Edinburgh (2018)
9. Cheng, P.: Decoding the rise of central bank digital currency in china: designs, problems, and prospects. J. Bank. Regul. **24**(2), 156–170 (2023)
10. Davoodalhosseini, M., Rivadeneyra, F., Zhu, Y.: CBDC and monetary policy. Tech. rep, Bank of Canada (2020)
11. Duffie, D.: Digital currencies and fast payment systems: disruption is coming. In: Asian Monetary Forum, May, Mimeo (2019)
12. Government, F.R.: Federal reserve chair jerome h. powell outlines the federal reserve's response to technological advances driving rapid change in the global payments landscape (2021). https://www.federalreserve.gov/newsevents/pressreleases/other20210520b.htm
13. Kenji, H., Hiroyuki, T., C.M.T.Y: Summary of the report of the study group on legal issues regarding central bank digital currency (2019). https://www.boj.or.jp/en/research/wps_rev/lab/lab19e03.htm
14. Jagtiani, J., Papaioannou, M., Tsetsekos, G., Dolson, E., Milo, D.: Cryptocurrencies: regulatory perspectives and implications for investors. In: The Palgrave Handbook of Technological Finance, pp. 161–186 (2021)
15. Jim, P.: White house considers creating a digital dollar (investopedia) (2022). https://www.investopedia.com/inside-the-new-white-house-framework-for-regulating-digital-assets-6674517
16. Kim, Y.S., Kwon, O.: Central bank digital currency and financial stability. Bank of Korea WP 6 (2019)
17. Kosse, A., Mattei, I.: Making headway-results of the 2022 BIS survey on central bank digital currencies and crypto. BIS Papers (2023)

18. Kshetri, N., Loukoianova, E.: Data privacy considerations for central bank digital currencies in asia-pacific countries. Computer **55**(03), 95–100 (2022)
19. Kumhof, M., Noone, C.: Central bank digital currencies-design principles and balance sheet implications (2018)
20. Nakamoto, S.: Bitcoin: a peer-to-peer electronic cash system. Decentralized Business Review (2008)
21. Náñez Alonso, S.L., Jorge-Vazquez, J., Reier Forradellas, R.F.: Central banks digital currency: detection of optimal countries for the implementation of a CBDC and the implication for payment industry open innovation. J. Open Innov. Technol. Market Complex. **7**(1) (2021). https://www.mdpi.com/2199-8531/7/1/72
22. Niepelt, D.: Monetary policy with reserves and CBDC: optimality, equivalence, and politics (2020)
23. NPP: NPP roadmap October 2022 (2022). https://tinyurl.com/2p9pn2y8. Accessed 30 July 2023
24. Ozili, P.K.: CBDC, fintech and cryptocurrency for financial inclusion and financial stability. In: Digital Policy, Regulation and Governance (ahead-of-print) (2022)
25. RBA. Strategic review of innovation in the payments system: conclusions (2012). https://www.rba.gov.au/payments-and-infrastructure/payments-system-regulation/past-regulatory-reviews/strategic-review-of-innovation-in-the-payments-system/. Accessed 02 July 2023
26. Rennie, E., Steele, S.: Privacy and emergency payments in a pandemic: how to think about privacy and a central bank digital currency. Law Technol. Hum. **3**(1), 6–17 (2021)
27. ReserveBankofAustralia. Research project exploring use cases for CBDC (2023). https://www.rba.gov.au/media-releases/2023/mr-23-06.html
28. Wang, H.: China's approach to central bank digital currency: selectively reshaping international financial order? Univ. Pennsylvania Asian Law Rev. **18**(1), 77 (2022)
29. Ward, O., Rochemont, S.: Understanding central bank digital currencies (CBDC). In: Institute and Faculty of Actuaries, pp. 1–52 (2019)
30. Xu, J.: Developments and implications of central bank digital currency: the case of china e-CNY. Asian Econ. Policy Rev. **17**(2), 235–250 (2022)
31. Yifei, F.: Some thoughts on CBDC operations in china. centralbanking.com. (1 April 2020)

Understanding Real-Time Payment Dynamics in Australia

Babu Pillai[✉][iD]

Southern Cross University, Gold Coast, Australia
pillai.babu@outlook.com

Abstract. While digital payments have transformed e-commerce, they are not without drawbacks. The most noticeable issues arise from extended payment settlement times and the costs incurred from card fees, largely due to reliance on credit card payment networks. To address these shortfalls, real-time payments have been introduced by various central banks. Although real-time payment systems have been available for some time and present numerous advantages, their adoption in Australia is still limited. This paper provides an in-depth overview of Australia's real-time payment network architecture, the New Payment Platform (NPP), including details of its service products and presents several use cases. While the aim is to inspire further innovations in the payment system utilising the NPP platform, the paper also examines the reasons for the limited adoption of real-time payments despite their clear advantages over traditional digital payment methods.

Keywords: digital payment · real-time payment · fast payment · New Payment Platform · NPP · PayId · PayTo

1 Introduction

Digital payments, also known as electronic payments, are systems that transfer digital money from one account to another using digital payment technology [14]. This technology refers to various methods of making electronic transfers of money. Technological developments have enabled innovation in digital payment methods, from traditional card payments to contactless mobile wallets and wearables, to QR codes [12,17,22]. Easy access to digital devices and internet connectivity has created a convenient pathway to digital payments [3]. The pandemic has reshaped payment preferences, driving a surge in digital payment methods, especially mobile wallets, which are projected to grow globally [10,33].

Despite significant changes to the payment system technology, for many nations, the fundamental architecture of the payment system, which includes integration through third-party payment providers, has remained relatively unchanged for over two decades. It is vital that payment networks, that support the payment system, are primarily driven by corporate businesses like Visa or Master, which promote innovation on top of their network.

© The Author(s), under exclusive license to Springer Nature Singapore Pte Ltd. 2024
N. Dong et al. (Eds.): SDLT 2023, CCIS 1975, pp. 124–145, 2024.
https://doi.org/10.1007/978-981-97-0006-6_9

The current traditional payment system involves multiple intermediaries verifying the settlement processes that decelerate money transfers compared to the exchange of information which can occur almost instantly. One might question *why the movement of money is slower than the speed of the information transfer.* Considering today's digital age, data globally can be transferred within seconds, yet traditional financial transactions often rely on intermediaries and may not settle for days.

1.1   Payment Settlement Time

The payment industry constantly innovates and enhances user experience by providing a variety of convenient options. However, the ability to settle business-to-business (B2B) and business-to-consumer (B2C) transactions depends on various clearing and settlement infrastructures. Unlike messages that transfer directly from sender to recipient, digital money must often pass through multiple hands. This includes the sender's bank, the clearing house, and the recipient's bank. Each intermediary can introduce delays. Card providers who profit from the transaction processing fees, dominate the clearing and settlement infrastructures landscape [31].

Credit card adoption and usage in most Western countries have been historically dominant. In most western countries, retail and business payment systems are dominated by credit card providers. The convenience offered by credit cards resonates with consumer-driven demand, thus supporting the dominance of the credit card industry over the payment system. Moreover, credit card companies often incentivise customers with rewards, cashback, and other benefits to keep the customers engaged [8]. As a result, businesses are compelled to use merchant terminals that are compatible with credit cards. Debit card transactions are often treated as credit card transactions because they utilise the same credit card processing systems.

Although consumers use debit cards to access their own funds, when making payments at a terminal enabled for credit card transactions, the transaction is processed through the credit card payment network. This means that even a debit transaction is routed through the system typically used for credit card transactions, including a processing fee. This raises the question: *Why does it cost money to use your own money?*

1.2   Payment Cost-to-Cost Money Exchange

Payment cost refers to the expenses as fees associated with financial transactions. Payment costs are based on the payment method of the service provider [15]. Card network providers typically charge a service flat fee of 3% regardless of based on credit or debit transaction. When making a digital payment with your debit card, the choice of network used to process the transaction can depend on the merchant provider. If the card network is Visa or Mastercard, the treatment of the transaction remains the same, regardless of type of the account (credit or debit).

Contactless payments such as payWave [35] and PayPass [13] use the same network as credit card transactions; therefore, a card surcharge is applied to that transaction regardless of card type such as credit or debit. For example, Aldi supermarket in Australia charges a 0.5% surcharge for contactless payments made with a Mastercard or Visa debit card [2]. Within the Queensland Department of Transport and Main Roads, all payments made with a credit or debit card incur a credit card surcharge [32].

Digital payments have gained wide adoption as a standard way in businesses. While digital payments offer convenience, transactions must go through network providers' systems. Customers have no choice but to agree to the payment system network providers' fee structure. Digital payments have many advantages, such as easy accessibility to funds 24/7 through online providers and are convenient to use. However, these benefits come with associated costs. Historically, banks have charged fees for providing safe custody of cash and maintaining security measures for cash storage in branches and ATMs. With technological advancements, banking transactions have become more automated, resulting in reduced human involvement and reduced physical branches for banks and ATMs [16]. Technological advancements have enabled more payment transactions to be carried out electronically, greatly benefiting the e-commerce industry. As more banking services have become electronic, the need for physical money has declined. While this reduces costs associated with the need for physical infrastructure, it increases costs related to network service. One such cost is the fee charged by payment network providers. Banks and Fintech companies often pass the payment network providers' service charges to their customers [34].

1.3 Problem Definition

In the evolving financial landscape, traditional payment and settlement systems present numerous challenges that hinder efficiency and transparency. These systems often incur delayed settlement times, with some transactions taking several days to complete, thereby posing cash flow challenges for businesses and individuals. Coupled with this is the issue of service charges. The involvement of multiple intermediaries in conventional systems often inflates the cost of transactions, with users sometimes unaware of the full extent of these fees, particularly in cases involving credit card surcharges. Furthermore, these traditional platforms frequently operate within a set of hours, leading to transaction delays if initiated outside of these time frames or during weekends. On the horizon, *real-time payment* systems promise *real-time* or *near-real-time* settlement at potentially lower costs [4,27]. However, their effectiveness hinges on widespread adoption, interoperability with existing systems, stringent security measures against potential fraud, compliance with ever-evolving financial regulations, and, ultimately, the trust of businesses and consumers. The core issue lies in determining the viability and advantages of transitioning from established payment mechanisms to these emerging fast payment systems while acknowledging and addressing inherent challenges.

The main contributions of this paper include:

- A comprehensive overview of digital payments and their associated components.
- An in-depth exploration of the real-time payment system.
- A review of the Australian real-time payment system, NPP, and its architecture.
- Insights into the adoption of real-time payment systems in Australia.

Real-time payment systems (RTPs) usually emphasise the immediate transfer of existing funds, although credit mechanisms can be integrated. The practicality of using credit with RTPs depends on bank policies, system rules, and regulations. This research solely examines debit money, excluding credit money.

2   Real-Time Payment System

A payment system refers to a set of processes, technologies, and infrastructure that allows businesses and individuals to make financial transactions. This typically happens through a financial provider. The entities involved in a payment system are the *payee, payer, banks*, and payment *network providers*.

Banks are regulated financial institutions that provide various services, including payment services. In this research, we limit our focus to electronic payment services, also called digital payments. The current banking industry is a multi-million-dollar business that settles business transactions through its network and plays a crucial role in the functioning of the economy. Banks provide payment services through various network provider's infrastructure, generally known as payment rail.

A *payment rail* is a network infrastructure that connects various financial institutions and provides a means for facilitating financial transactions. The most predominant payment rails include Mastercard, Visa, Discover, and American Express. Banks use payment rails as the underlying infrastructure to process, settle, and transfer funds for various types of financial transactions. The electronic card issued by a bank to its customers carries the label or logo of the network provider that the bank utilises as a payment rail. This label indicates that the card can be used within the network's payment system, enabling customers to transact and transfer their funds through that specific payment rail.

2.1   Payment System Workflow

Let us define the bank that debits an amount from the payer known as the *issuer* and the payee's bank, which credits the amount on the receipt is the *acquirer* and the payment network provider as *card network*.

Figure 1 shows a simplified transaction flow of a payment system that begins with the customer paying using a payment card at the merchant's point-of-sale (PoS) system. The PoS machine sends the authorisation request to the acquiring bank [29][1], which then routes it through the card provider's card network [9][2]

---

[1] A bank or financial institution that processes credit or debit card payments on behalf of a merchant.

[2] An organisation that facilitates payment card transactions.

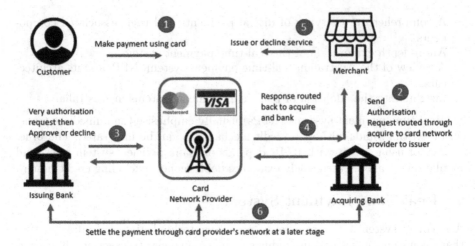

Fig. 1. Simplified architecture of a card payment system.

to the issuer bank [29][3] for approval. The issuer bank verifies the authorisation request, the customer's account details, available funds, and other relevant factors. Based on this information, the issuer's bank clears the transaction by approving or declining it. This response is then transmitted back through the card provider's network to the acquiring bank and the merchant. The PoS prints a receipt if approved, and the merchant can provide the product. Otherwise, the merchant may decline the service or arrange an alternative payment method. After the transaction is completed, the acquiring bank initiates the settlement process through the card provider's network to transfer the funds from the customer's account to the merchant's account.

2.2 Payment Network Provider

A payment network provider is a company or organisation that offers services related to processing payment transactions. They typically handle the technical aspects of payment processing, including managing the network infrastructure that facilitates transactions between various parties involved in the payment ecosystem. Additionally, payment network providers often implement security measures and fraud prevention mechanisms to protect against fraudulent activities and ensure the integrity of the payment network.

Visa and Mastercard are prominent payment network providers for electronic transactions among merchants, cardholders (users), and financial institutions. Banks issue cards to customers, embedding them with compatibility for Visa or Mastercard readers. Merchants employ card reader devices that connect to the Visa and Mastercard networks, enabling payment processing. It is important to note that, over the past five decades, the fundamental structure of the payment

---

[3] Bank that provides cards to consumers.

system, where banks keep their own ledger and payment network providers synchronise this ledger, has remained largely unchanged, except for advancements at the periphery, such as contactless payments.

The business model of payment network providers is to earn revenue through transaction fees. Transaction fees are typically a small percentage of the value of the transaction or a fixed fee value. These fees are generally referred to as *surcharges* and are typically charged to the acquiring bank by the payment network provider for using the service.

2.3   Payment Surcharge

A payment surcharge is an extra fee that businesses can charge customers for using a digital payment system [11,34]. It is the actual costs businesses incur to accept payment using the service of a payment network card provider [6]. Depending on the merchant agreement and card type, businesses are charged for using digital payment services. The amount it costs a business to process a payment will depend on factors such as the size of the business, the technology used to process payments, and the payment method. Small businesses may have higher processing costs than larger ones, and the cost to smaller businesses may be higher [1].

In theory, by adding surcharges to offset their expenses, merchants might reduce the prices of products and services for buyers. Some businesses decide not to charge payment surcharges. Instead, they factor the cost into the price of their goods and services, which would apply to all customers. Regardless of how the business recovers costs, the customer must bear the cost of using card payments [18]. The banks' payment service, using this third-party card service, the burden of processing payments is no longer an overhead for banks; and for businesses, passing third-party service card fees to customers reduces their expenses. Customers have a choice of using their preferred payment type at their expense. Customers may prefer businesses which are not pass card surcharges during payment process. This became a challenge for small businesses that pass card surcharges directly back to their customers [24].

For Australian consumers, when dealing with businesses that use the Visa or Mastercard payment service, a possible alternative to avoid surcharges is to opt for cash payments. However, use of cash for day-to-day transactions has been declining in Australia for many years [16]. This trend has implications for all aspects of the cash system, including the mechanisms supporting cash distribution and accessibility. Notably, a majority of banks now host ATM services solely within their premises [28]. Moreover, many public ATMs, particularly those in shopping centres, levy a withdrawal charge.

2.4   Digital Payment - Discussion

Digital cards, such as credit or debit cards, provide convenience and ease of transaction for individuals and businesses. The use of digital cards is generally viewed as a socially beneficial practice. The additional cost associated with digital card payments is often considered a convenience fee; thus, businesses recover the expenses of processing such payments. However, it is important to note that many customers may not fully comprehend the fact that *they are essentially paying for the convenience of using their own money in electronic debit card payments.*

Even though we migrated from cash to cheques and to digital payment, traditional payment still takes a day or longer to clear, and the speed of electronic bank transfers depends on a country's banking infrastructure. Traditionally, they have been processed in large batches once or several times a day and did not process electronic payments at night or on weekends. This can have a significant effect on business, especially for small businesses that rely on receiving payments promptly to support their cash flow.

Countries worldwide are investing in their banking infrastructure to help money move faster, bringing the benefits of the digital economy to more people and businesses. As a result, an infrastructure has emerged called *RTPs*, also known as *instant payments*, *faster payments* or *immediate payments*. The rest of the paper refers to this as RTPs.

3   Real Time Payment System (RTPs)

RTPs refers to a payment system that transfers funds in real time and provides immediate availability of funds to its recipient. When an RTP transaction is authorised, the payer's account balance is instantly deducted, and the recipient receives a confirmation of funds in real-time. While the settlement timing may vary between different payment schemes, it typically takes only a few seconds to complete.

RTPs payments are one of the most significant financial innovations in the past decade [5]. RTPs services enable financial institutions to offer efficient, instant payment services in real-time, either free of charge in some nations or with a small fee in others. These services have proven benefits in driving digital adoption, financial inclusion, and boosting small business economies, in many nations.

An important aspect of RTPs systems is the *speed of settlement* and its *associated cost*. Typically, a payee will take a day or more to receive funds using a traditional payment system network, while RTPs systems can execute transactions in real-time. Real-time payments use a different network rail facilitated by central bank partnerships, prioritising payment services and removing the intermediaries, which reduces the time and costs associated with settlements. Efforts to develop and provide RTPs networks vary across the globe. Most of the development is initiated by central banks collaborating with financial institutions, industry providers, and technology companies. These entities work together to develop and offer RTPs networks that are cost-effective and more convenient compared to traditional payment network providers such as Visa or MasterCard.

3.1   Functionalities: RTPs vs traditional payment

In traditional card payments, the payee's point-of-sale (PoS) terminal initiates the payment transaction flow when a payer uses their card. The terminal sends the transaction details to the acquiring bank's network, which then forwards them to the card provider (such as Visa or Mastercard). The card provider routes the transaction to the issuer bank for clearance. Once the issuer bank approves the transaction, the payer receives the product or service, and the acquiring bank initiates the settlement process.

In RTPs, the payment flow is reversed. The payer initiates the transaction to pay the payee and sends the payment details through the payer's bank to the RTPs network. The network checks the payer's credentials, verifies the payee's details, and, if they exist, processes the settlement immediately on behalf of their bank. The payer is notified of the result, and the funds are transferred from the payer's account to the payee's account and to their relevant banks in real-time. The key distinction is that in traditional card payments, the payment communication flows from the payee to the payer through various intermediaries. Whereas, in RTPs, the communication flows directly from the payer to the payee, allowing for immediate settlement and notification of the transaction result. The payer authorises the payment, which is deducted from their account and made available to the beneficiary immediately through the real-time payment network.

3.2   Business Model for RTPs

The business model of RTPs varies depending on the parties involved. Those initiated or overseen by the central bank or government prioritise broader societal benefits over direct revenue generation. In such instances, funding for the network's development and operation may come from government budgets or financial support from the central bank. The systems that are developed through financial institutions' partnerships may generate revenue through transaction fees for payments processed through the system.

In both cases, the main objectives of RTPs are to provide seamless payment services across participating financial institutions (banks). To achieve this, banks must integrate RTPs into their existing banking systems and offer their services to their customers. The entities that own and operate RTPs and their services differ in each country. A global RTPs tracker website[4] by the World Bank aims to provide a consolidated and comprehensive overview of the status of implementation of RTPs worldwide.

4   RTPs in Australia

In 2012, the Reserve Bank of Australia (RBA) published strategic objectives for the Australian payment system and invited the industry to determine the most effective way to deliver payment services. In [26] response, an industry

---

[4] https://fastpayments.worldbank.org/global-tracker.

committee proposed to develop a new, purpose-built payment infrastructure. In 2014, twelve institutions committed to fund and construct a new domestic payment infrastructure, launched in 2018 as New Payments Platform [25].

4.1 New Payments Platform

The New Payments Platform (NPP) is an open-access payment platform that enables Australian financial institutions to leverage their services of real-time, inter-bank payment service to their customers. The NPP platform supports financial institutions and service providers to develop overlay services on the NPP for innovative payment services to its end-users. NPP can be considered as or going to be Australia's national payments infrastructure owned by a consortium of financial institutions and operated by NPP Australia Limited[5] under the guidance of the Reserve Bank of Australia.

The architecture of NPP comprises three distinct layers: *Governance*, *Functional*, and *Application*. The governance layer provides strategic oversight and direction, encompassing policies, standards, and frameworks that guide the decisions of the systems. It delegates roles, responsibilities, and accountability mechanisms, ensuring compliance with both internal and external requirements. The functional layer, representing a distinct software stratum, delivers specific functionalities, translating the strategic directives from the governance layer into actionable processes and routines. The application layer comprises tools, software applications, and technologies designed to support and facilitate the functional processes.

While the governance layer determines *why* and *what* regarding strategic objectives and policies, the functional layer dictates *how* regarding processes and workflows. Meanwhile, the application layer equips the system with the technological tools required to implement those processes. The points below provide an in-depth look at various elements within each NPP's composing layers.

– **Governance**: The governance layer comprises the governance organisation, the Australian Payments Plus (AP+), formally known as NPP Australia. It comprises thirteen financial institutions referred to as participants. Other parties can subscribe and pay a fee to be part of this network or be sponsored by one of the thirteen financial institutions.
– **Functional**: The functional layer consist of *Fast Settlement Service*, *Basic Infrastructure* and *PayID Addressing Service*.
  • Fast Settlement Service: The fast settlement service is operated by the Reserve Bank of Australia, clearing and settling RTPs transactions. All thirteen financial institutions have access to the service for balancing liquidity and maintaining ledgers.
  • Basic Infrastructure: The basic infrastructure is developed by SWIFT and based on the international messaging standard ISO 20022 [19] messaging construct which facilitates the exchange of messages between counterparties in a modern standard for routing messages (Fig. 2).

---

[5] https://nppa.com.au/.

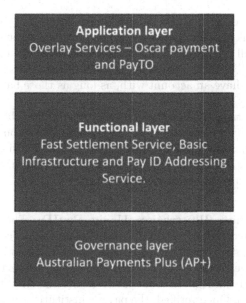

Fig. 2. Architecture of NPP.

- Pay ID Addressing Service: This is a centralised addressing service, extending the ability to address payments through an identifier such as mobile numbers, ABN, etc.
- **Application**: The application layer is referred as Overlay Services in the NPP ecosystem. These services sit on top of the NPP functional layer to facilitate faster payments. Current overlay services are *Osko* payment and *PayTo*.

Within the functional layer, the technical details of the 'fast settlement service' and 'basic infrastructure' are irrelevant to this research. These software services are already built, and only the functional aspects of these services are pertinent to this discussion. Therefore, the technical details about these services have been omitted. At a high level, with the NPP system, validation and confirmation of the payment instructions are undertaken before instructing the settlement layer; therefore, settlement can be carried out when cross-checking. Subsequently, the payer bank instigates settlement by sending settlement instructions to the NPP system. The instructions are processed by a functional layer in which the actual movement of funds between the bank accounts occurs in the NPP ledger on a 24/7/365 basis. In this process, the beneficiary bank can immediately post the funds to the beneficiary's account.

4.2 PayId

PayID is a digital identifier unique to a user and serves as a link to their bank account. The identifier can be a phone number, email address, or Australian

Business Number (ABN). PayID can only be registered to the NPP network by a participating bank on behalf of its consumers[6]. Once registered, the PayID is recognised across all participating financial institutions within the NPP ecosystem. Users can use PayID to recognise themself in the NPP network, regardless of which bank they have an account with, as long as those banks are part of the NPP ecosystem.

The main advantage of using PayID is that it simplifies the payment process. Instead of sharing bank details, such as the BSB code, account number, name, or bank name, users only need to share their PayID identifier. This makes the process of accepting and making payments more convenient and secure, as the sensitive bank account information remains private.

A Simple Workflow Illustration Using PayID: The payment process begins with the payer initiating the payment using the payee's PayID through a banking channel, such as an online banking portal or mobile application. An enquiry is sent to the PayID addressing service, which returns the payee's. PayID account details and the legal account name associated with the PayID for the payer's confirmation. Once verified, the payer's institution sends a payment message, including all relevant transaction details, to the payee's institution through NPP rails for confirmation. After the payee's institution confirms its ability to credit the payee's account through any NPP integrated services such as Osko, it initiates the settlement in real-time between both banks.

4.3 Osko Payment

Osko by BPAY is the first overlay service on NPP in Australia. It is a payment service that allows consumers to transfer money almost instantly from one bank to another using PayID. Osko operates as an application built on top of the NPP rail, allowing for RTPs between different banks. Users can pay individuals or businesses using one of two identifiers: their PayID or their traditional account details (BSB and account number). The Osko service is widely used by banks for their pay-anyone feature, enabling customers to make instant payments to other parties. After processing payment using Osko, users may notice the Osko logo (Osko ◎) pop-up indicating that the transaction has been successfully completed.

4.4 PayTo

PayTo is an advanced payment system that addresses several limitations and challenges associated with traditional direct debit transactions. PayTo introduces a feature that lets both consumers and businesses customise payment parameters. Users can define consent for payment, select the source account, specify the payment amount, and decide the duration of the payment agreement. Consumers using PayTo enjoy greater control over their bank account

---

[6] https://payid.com.au/faqs/.

payments and can oversee them securely through their current desktop or mobile banking interfaces. For businesses, the platform eliminates the unpredictability of bank account payments, reducing wait times for potential dishonours and cutting administrative expenses.

The PayTo payment system can be used for bills, memberships, and subscription services. It provides a broad, scalable, and secure solution for third-party payment initiation, including:

- Immediate notification of payment declines: Unlike the traditional system, where direct debit transactions might be dishonoured, and the concerned party might only find out much later, PayTo notifies billers immediately if a payment does not go through. This immediate feedback can prevent consumers from incurring fees associated with bounced or dishonoured debits.
- Centralised authority: PayTo operates with a centralised system, making it possible to modify payment details in real time. Any change a customer makes is communicated quickly, ensuring all involved parties are aware.
- Certainty for consumers: With PayTo, consumers no longer have to deal with the ambiguity of when their payments will be processed. This system ensures that consumers know exactly when their money will be deducted.
- Enhanced security: PayTo's closed-loop solution prioritises security. Payment details, particularly sensitive ones like card expiration dates, remain confidential, reducing the risk of potential misuse or fraud.
- Efficient cancellation process: If a user wants to cancel a direct debit, the request is processed promptly with PayTo, ensuring the customer's wishes are respected and implemented promptly.

Utilising the RTPs capabilities of the NPP and PayTo facilitates payments directly from bank accounts, accommodating both one-off purchases and regular recurring payments. Key features include instant settlement, immediate account validation, notifications, enhanced security, and integrated payment schedules. Moreover, it supports extensive transactional data. This service benefits various stakeholders: Organisations receive payments for goods and services more efficiently, businesses that outsource payroll get faster money movement, and FinTech entities can capitalise on rapid fund transfers.

A Simple Workflow Illustration of PayTo: Consider the example of a real estate business. Traditionally, when such a business collects rent from their tenants, there is a waiting period of two to three business days before they can confirm whether a payment has been successfully processed. With the PayTo solution, real estate businesses have the capability to debit rents from the tenants' bank accounts instantly. The real-time nature of this service ensures that if a payment fails, the business is notified without delay, eliminating the typical two to three-day waiting period. For tenants, this translates into immediate notification of the transaction's status. In the event of a failed transaction, they can arrange for an alternative payment method promptly, thereby avoiding potential dishonour or overdraft fees imposed by their bank or service provider.

4.5   Difference Osko and PayTo

Using Osko payment, users can pay or get paid to their linked bank account, whereas PayTo enables a way to collect payments in real-time directly from another account. In other words, PayTo is a way for businesses or merchants to collect real-time payments from a user's account. With PayTo, the business starts the payment process, and the user's bank checks transaction details based on the pre-authorised PayTo agreement the user has signed. In other words, with Osko, the payer initiates the payment to the payee, whereas with PayTo, a payee can ask for payment from the payer's account.

4.6   Potential Benefits and Use Case of RTPs

As the financial landscape evolves, the potential benefits of RTPs come into sharper focus, offering transformative use cases that cater to modern demands.

Peer-to-Peer Payment: With Osko and PayID, the Peer-to-Peer (P2P) payment process becomes seamless and efficient. P2P payments can add convenience to everyday transactions, like splitting a bill or sending money to a friend or relative. There are a range of scenarios where P2P payment is very useful. As we move away from cash transactions, P2P payment become increasingly common and widely adopted.

Payments for Day-to-Day Use: Currently, many individuals rely on their day-to-day earnings to cover immediate expenses such as groceries, petrol, and food. These average income earners typically work shifts and require quick access to their wages to meet their immediate needs. RTPs enables employers to pay wages instantly after completing the shift. This offers financial flexibility to users as they can immediately use the money, they earned for their everyday expenses without relying on credit card providers.

Payments for Business Transactions: RTPs payments offer several advantages for a business to manage their cash flow effectively. Merchants will receive immediate settlement for point-of-sale transactions, allowing them to pay their suppliers promptly, ensuring a smoother supply chain process, paying wages and other business expenses quickly, and enhancing customer trust.

Small Business Transactions: For small businesses, the current Osko PayID has several benefits such as i) instant payments: allows small businesses to receive payments from customers almost instantly. ii) Cost-effective payment solutions: Transactions often have no or lower costs than traditional payment methods, making them cost-effective for small businesses and customers. Osko PayID is a valuable tool for small businesses, enabling them to offer their customers efficient and convenient payment options and improve their overall financial operations.

Organisational Benefit: With the current payment system, businesses wanting to pay their employees must deposit the amount a few days ahead. For example, if the employees are to be paid on a Monday, the employer must deposit the amount on Wednesday or Thursday for the payment to be credited to the employees' accounts. That requires a 4-day advance, including the weekend. During these 4 days, the money is not in the account of either the employer or the employee. However, with RTPs payment, the employer can automate the payment to be deducted on Sunday, Saturday, or Monday morning or evening. This way, the money is not floating around somewhere.

These use cases demonstrate how an RTPs benefits both users and businesses by ensuring rapid and efficient access to funds, fostering a seamless financial experience for all participants. However, RTPs features need to be made available to users and businesses through banking channels and payment service providers.

4.7   Discussion

The two main features of instant and low or no-cost transactions attract the adoption of RTPs because it benefits business and their customers. RTPs services are easier for banks and other financial institutions to adopt and remove the development of technological burden. RTPs speeds up the payment process for domestic transactions. RTPs are already set up for cross-border payments between some countries [21]. CBDCs and stablecoins could be the technologies that will compete with RTPs to be the future of digital payment systems.

In most countries that successfully adopted RTPs, such as India, Brazil and Thailand, central banking has been involved in developing the RTPs framework and providing regulatory oversight over the network. At the time of writing this paper, Australia's RTPs, NPP, were and are in the hands of commercial banking participants. While Central banks oversee the regulation and operation of the network. A most attractive use case is peer-to-peer payments, in which people directly pay one another from their bank accounts via an app. This is extremely useful because it happens instantly at no cost (as of 2023). The features of PayTo make it easier and faster for people to pay bills, make payments on delivery or make payments on e-commerce marketplaces directly from their bank account. Several payment service companies are developing products integrating PayTo with business applications at a comparatively lower cost than traditional card networks.

5   Adoption of RTPs in Australia

A recent survey results from BIS [20] notes that 70% of central banks already have RTPs in place with varied degrees of success in adoption. The adoption has varied dramatically by country and who promotes it. One key factor that drives adoption is the involvement of central banks and mandatory banking partnerships to provide real-time service. The low transaction fee was another enabling factor for adoption.

A 2022 NPP roadmap report [23] shows that close to 89 million accounts can make or receive RTPs payments. NPP accounts for approximately 30% of account-to-account or push-based payment processes and an average of 100 million monthly transactions. By 2030, NPP is projected to become the preferred payment system for both consumer and business transactions.

As of 2023, most banks offer two types of Osko payment services: personal banking and business accounts. Osko payment has been integrated into banking apps as a standout feature for everyday financial activities. Users can easily access and utilise Osko's features directly through their regular banking apps. However, RTPs applications such as Osko and PayTo are not widely available for business operations. For any business, the payment system they adopt needs to integrate seamlessly into their operations; otherwise, it might create operational inefficiencies, leading to potential errors or delays. One significant task for business accounting is payment reconciliation - ensuring that the amounts received match sales or invoices. Without integration, reconciling payments made via RTPs can become labour-intensive, increasing the potential for errors.

5.1   RTPs Service Providers

Several Australian companies are developing RTPs solutions for businesses, organisations and governments, offering various services such as PayID for businesses, PayTo for billers, and eCommerce accounting solutions (Table 1).

Table 1. RTPs providers

Name	Website
Azupay	https://www.azupay.com.au/
Zepto	https://www.zepto.com.au/
Monoova	https://www.monoova.com/
Eway	https://www.eway.com.au/

The business model of these RTPs service providers primarily revolves around generating revenue through transaction fees. In many ways, they operate similarly to credit card providers (they leverage NPP rails instead of credit card rails). The service product could be banks offering bundled services, including a payment terminal, gateway, or e-commerce systems that integrate with existing sales systems belonging to third-party RTPs service providers. Some of these RTPs providers may also adopt a Software-as-a-Service (SaaS) [30] model, levying regular fees on businesses for platform usage. For end users, this prompts questions about whether the benefits of instant payments could be overshadowed by the costs associated with these services. Comparing the fee structures across various RTP service providers and benchmarking them against conventional credit card services is a topic worth exploring in future research.

5.2   Observations

It has been evident that many people use the Osko payment for personal transactions through their banking app; however, it is not present in business and merchants' payment offerings to the best of our knowledge as of 2023. Recently, several news reports in the media have been about merchants struggling with the rise in costs and discussions about transaction fees. According to many small businesses, they cannot bear the card surcharge fee, so they pass it on to the customers. At the same time, they are worried that this factor may drive customers to merchants that do not charge a surcharge fee. The elephant in the room in this conversation is the transaction fee. Interestingly, none of the conversations about card payments or surcharges mentions Osko payments. *Is this because the public and small businesses are unaware of it?*

Why Are Small Businesses Not Using Osko Payment?: Let us assume that small businesses adopt digital payment methods due to customer demand. They subscribe to point-of-sale card terminals through their banking partner. In a society where card payments are predominantly used, it is challenging for businesses to make a change. In this situation, businesses have no incentive or benefit to transition to Osko unless there is a demand from the customer side. Additionally, there may be a lack of awareness or understanding of using the Osko feature for small businesses because Osko payment processes are not integrated into the PoS card terminals or gateway systems (as of 2023). Therefore, receiving payments using PayID is a manual process that involves providing the PayID to customers and ensuring the payment has been received. Without proper training or informational sessions, which small businesses might not have the resources to access, they may not see the value in offering it. This inertia and resistance to change are not uncommon, especially when businesses are content with their existing payment methods.

Use Case for Osko Payment System: Small Scale Businesses: With some modifications to the banking apps, small businesses could utilise Osko payment for retail transactions. For P2P payments with Osko, users must manually exchange their PayID details. This manual process is time-consuming for businesses and can lead to errors. If banks could introduce a feature that allows the reading of PayID details from a QR code, and if merchants provided their PayID details by making it easier, such as a QR code, users could then use their existing banking apps to scan the code. This would auto-fill the merchant's details, allowing users to simply enter the amount and make the payment. This method aligns with how many QR code-based mobile payments currently operate.

This simple and elegant solution allows small scale businesses to utilise digital payments without transaction fees. As of 2023, Osko payments are free for both the sender and recipient (there is no information about whether Osko for business payments includes a fee or not). Even though this seems like a straightforward solution, to the best of our knowledge, no banks currently offer this QR code scanning feature, and none of the payment service providers are developing an app to offer this free service.

Why Banks Are Not Promoting It?: Banks have not been motivated to promote RTPs, primarily because their established infrastructure built around credit card rails has served them effectively for decades. This infrastructure provides them with predictable revenue streams, especially from transaction fees and associated services. Moreover, with its established clients and global acceptance, the credit card system offers banks a comfort zone that RTPs might disrupt. Thus, unless there is a distinct competitive advantage or a strong demand from their customer base, many banks do not see an immediate need to promote RTPs.

5.3   Consumer Behaviour

Consumers' adoption of RTPs has been somewhat tempered by deeply ingrained habits and the allure of credit card reward systems. Credit card companies have invested heavily in loyalty programs, offering points, miles, cashback, and other incentives that have become deeply embedded in the consumer psyche. These incentives encourage the continued use of credit cards and make them more appealing compared to newer payment systems that might not offer such perks. For many consumers, the immediate benefit of earning rewards outweighs the potential advantages of RTPs, such as faster transaction times. Additionally, the familiarity and trust built over years of using credit cards create a sense of comfort, making it challenging for RTPs to break this stronghold, even if they promise better efficiency or lower fees. The inertia in consumer behaviour, driven by the allure of credit card benefits and established trust in traditional systems, poses a substantial challenge to the widespread adoption of RTPs.

5.4   Strategic Drivers for the Adoption of RTPs

In the evolving financial landscape, RTPs presents a transformative approach to instant monetary transactions. However, their widespread adoption hinges on various strategic drivers. Among them are providing incentives, mandates from central banks, and leading by example at the government level. These are just a few examples, and there could be other strategies as well.

Providing Incentives: Incentivising businesses and organisations to adopt RTPs can significantly accelerate their integration and usage across various sectors. Drawing from successful models like India, where the government introduced monetary incentives for businesses adopting digital payment, was a very successful strategy. Additionally, governments can collaborate with banks to offer special terms for businesses adopting RTPs. On the consumer side, discounts, cashback, or loyalty points can be offered to encourage the frequent use of RTPs for everyday transactions. By creating a financially advantageous environment for businesses and consumers to use RTPs, governments can ensure quicker adoption and a smoother transition away from traditional payment systems.

Central Bank Mandates: Central bank mandates can significantly drive RTPs adoption. When central banks mandate the adoption of RTPs, it is a powerful catalyst to accelerate the integration and usage of these systems within the banking infrastructure. Central banks, being the primary monetary authorities, possess the leverage to enforce regulations and standards that the broader financial sector must adhere to. A mandate from the central bank signals the critical importance and urgency of RTPs implementation to the entire financial community. Such directives typically arise from modernising payment infrastructures, enhancing financial inclusion, improving transaction efficiency, and meeting consumer demands for immediate payment solutions.

Government Leads by Example: Government-led initiatives often set the tone for broader market transformations. By adopting RTPs for all its services, including welfare payments, the government can create a precedent and a model for other sectors to emulate. Given the substantial volume of transactions that governments handle daily, their adoption of RTPs can significantly raise the system's visibility and familiarity among the general public. This, in turn, can build trust and ease concerns about the new system's efficiency and reliability. When citizens experience the benefits of RTPs firsthand through government services, they are more likely to prefer it in other aspects of their financial transactions. This positive ripple effect can then facilitate a smoother transition for retail sectors to integrate and promote RTPs, as consumers would already be accustomed to the convenience and immediacy of such systems.

5.5 The Network Effect: How Adoption Challenges Grow with User Base

The network effect [7] is a phenomenon wherein a product or service gains its value as more people use it. Network effect poses adoption challenges with the RTPs. In the context of a RTPs, the platform's value will grow as more individuals and businesses adopt and use it for their transactions. The PayID system can create value for a RTPs ecosystem by bringing users together under a unified identifier system. As more users join and utilise PayIDs for payments, the platform becomes more valuable due to the network effects. This is like how social media platforms, like Facebook or WhatsApp, become more useful as more people join, interact, and connect with each other.

The unique dynamic of adoption economics is that when a platform has few users initially, potential users may hesitate to adopt it. They are more likely to join if they see others using it, creating a positive feedback loop. This makes it crucial for new systems to achieve critical mass early on to establish a strong presence in the market. With sufficient adoption, new platforms can compete effectively. Therefore, RTPs systems must address the network effects challenge by gaining traction and attracting a significant user base early. Establishing widespread adoption and acceptance of such systems among users and businesses is essential for the platform's long-term success in the evolving landscape of digital payment systems.

Despite their advantages, RTPs faces significant challenges in the credit card market. Firstly, establishing an RTPs demands substantial infrastructure investment and presents integration complexities for businesses already aligned with existing payment workflows. The inertia of both consumers and merchants used to establish payment methods further hinders adoption. Interoperability is another concern, as RTPs needs seamless integration with e-commerce systems. Moreover, the loyalty programs of credit cards, combined with the need for intensive marketing to educate potential RTPs users, make the task of broad adoption even more daunting. While RTPs offers innovation and potential cost savings, breaking into a market dominated by established credit card systems is difficult.

In RTPs payment adoption, the distinction between credit and debit money plays a significant role in influencing the adoption rate. Most Western nations predominantly utilise credit money, relying on systems that lend consumers money in advance to be repaid later. In contrast, many Asian countries primarily operate on debit money, where transactions are conducted using funds that are already available in a consumer's account. Given this context, integrating RTPs is comparatively easier in Asian countries than in Western nations, largely because the system aligns more closely with the region's prevailing financial behaviours and structures.

5.6   RTPs and Blockchain

The digital payment landscape is rapidly changing, with various players ranging from centralised systems like RTP to the decentralised Defi ecosystems. While decentralised platforms grapple with changing regulations, centralised RTPs may enjoy a brief respite. However, if decentralised platforms gain significant popularity, the demand for decentralised payment systems will surge. To stay competitive, traditional RTPs will need to diversify their services, prompting them to adapt to this ever-changing financial environment.

Blockchain technology has emerged as a revolutionary solution to numerous challenges in the payments industry. Initially, the primary application of blockchain centered around disintermediation, essentially reducing the role of intermediaries in financial transactions, thus fostering greater trust in the system. Additionally, it promised to make transactions more cost-effective and faster. As the technology evolved, its potential in enabling real-time settlements became evident, streamlining processes and reducing transaction times, especially for cross-border transactions. A distinction worth noting is between public blockchains and enterprise or permissioned blockchains. While public blockchains are open to all, enterprise chains are customisable and can be fine-tuned to address specific organisational needs and challenges. Consequently, they are particularly adept at tackling issues related to privacy and security in financial transactions. In essence, blockchain is suitability for redefining the payments landscape for decentralise ecosystem. The key to the success of these technologies is adoption, especially by retailers and businesses.

6   Conclusion

The benefit of real-time payment is very valuable; however, its full benefit may depend on the implementation of it through various financial institutions with the aim of providing maximum benefit to the end users. A significant portion of central banks have already implemented RTP systems, with their success in adoption being influenced by multiple factors. NPP's projection as the go-to payment system by 2030 further strengthens the narrative of RTPs being a cornerstone in future financial transactions. However, while there is evident adoption of personal banking, its penetration into business operations remains limited. To achieve widespread acceptance across both personal and commercial sectors, the next phase for RTP systems will undoubtedly focus on addressing these operational challenges, ensuring they become an indispensable tool in modern finance.

Acknowledgement. I would like to extend my heartfelt appreciation to Naveen Saxena (https://www.linkedin.com/in/naveen-saxena-21756854/), Kevin Naing (https://www.linkedin.com/in/kevin-naing-a0a02798/), and Zahid Farhan (https://www.linkedin.com/in/zahid-f-0a4aa323/) for their invaluable discussions concerning real-time payments in Australia. Their insights have immensely enriched this work. Further, my gratitude goes to Nathan Churchward (https://www.linkedin.com/in/nathanchurchward/) for providing constructive feedback on this paper, which greatly enhanced its quality.

References

1. Adams, D.: SMEs slogged with card transaction fees three times higher than big business, with least-cost routing yet to reach full potential. https://www.smartcompany.com.au/finance/cashflow/reserve-bank-australia-card-transaction-interchange-fees-speech/l. Accessed 02 Oct 2023
2. ALDI: Why is there a surcharge on contactless transactions? https://help.aldi.com.au/s/article/Why-is-there-a-surcharge-on-contactless-transactions?language=en_US. Accessed 02 Aug 2023
3. Augsburg, C., Hedman, J.: Value added services and adoption of mobile payments. In: Proceedings of the Sixteenth International Conference on Electronic Commerce, pp. 27–32 (2014)
4. Bech, M.L., Hancock, J.: Innovations in payments. BIS Q. Rev. (2020)
5. BIS: Innovations in retail payments (2012). https://www.bis.org/cpmi/publ/d102.pdf. Accessed 02 July 2023
6. Bolt, W., Chakravorti, S.: Economics of payment cards: a status report. Econ. Perspect. **32**(4) (2008)
7. Boudreau, K.J., Jeppesen, L.B.: Unpaid crowd complementors: the platform network effect mirage. Strateg. Manag. J. **36**(12), 1761–1777 (2015)

8. Bourguignon, H., Gomes, R., Tirole, J.: Shrouded transaction costs: must-take cards, discounts and surcharges. Int. J. Ind. Organ. **63**, 99–144 (2019)
9. Chakravorti, S.: Theory of credit card networks: a survey of the literature. Rev. Netw. Econ. **2**(2) (2003)
10. Chaudhari, C., Kumar, A.: Study of impact of the COVID-19 outbreak on digital payment in India. Vidyabharati Int. Interdiscip. Res. J. **12**(02), 99–102 (2021)
11. Dark, C., Fisher, C., McBey, K., Tellez, E.: Payment surcharges: economics, regulation and enforcement. RBA Bulletin, December, viewed 2 (2021)
12. De Kerviler, G., Demoulin, N.T., Zidda, P.: Adoption of in-store mobile payment: are perceived risk and convenience the only drivers? J. Retail. Consum. Serv. **31**, 334–344 (2016)
13. Debitcards: Mastercard paypass. https://www.debitcards.com.au/mastercard-paypass/. Accessed 02 Aug 2023
14. Franciska, A.M., Sahayaselvi, S.: An overview on digital payments. Int. J. Res. **4**(13), 2101–2111 (2017)
15. Frankel, A.S.: Monopoly and competition in the supply and exchange of money. Antitrust LJ **66**, 313 (1997)
16. Guttmann, R., Livermore, T., Zhang, Z.: The cash-use cycle in Australia. 1. 1 Renters, Rent Inflation and Renter Stress 2. Fixed-rate Housing Loans: Monetary Policy Transmission and Financial 10 Stability Risks 3. 19 A New Measure of Average Household Size 4. 27 Non-bank Lending in Australia and the Implications for Financial Stability, p. 39 (2023)
17. Hartmann, M., Hernandez, L., Plooij, M., Vandeweyer, Q.: Are instant retail payments becoming the new normal. A comparative study. Európai Központi Bank (2017)
18. Hayashi, F.: Discounts and surcharges: Implications for consumer payment choice. Federal Reserve Bank of Kansas City, Payments System Research Briefing, June 2012
19. Financial Infrastructure: Norges bank
20. Kosse, A., Mattei, I.: Making headway-results of the 2022 BIS survey on central bank digital currencies and crypto. BIS Papers (2023)
21. Monetary Authority of Singapore: Launch of real-time payments between Singapore and India (2023). https://tinyurl.com/mtm5dyam
22. Nguyen, T., Watson, B.: Consumer payment behaviour in Australia. RBA Bulletin, June (2023)
23. NPP: NPP roadmap October 2022 (2022). https://tinyurl.com/2p9pn2y8. Accessed 30 July 2023
24. Partsinevelos, K.: How small businesses are fighting inflated credit card swipe fees. https://www.cnbc.com/2023/02/09/small-businesses-credit-card-swipe-fees.html. Accessed 02 Oct 2023
25. RBA: The new payments platform. https://www.rba.gov.au/payments-and-infrastructure/new-payments-platform/. Accessed 02 Aug 2023
26. RBA: Strategic review of innovation in the payments system: Conclusions (2012). https://www.rba.gov.au/payments-and-infrastructure/payments-system-regulation/past-regulatory-reviews/strategic-review-of-innovation-in-the-payments-system/. Accessed 02 July 2023
27. Rysman, M., Schuh, S.: New innovations in payments. Innov. Policy Econ. **17**(1), 27–48 (2017)
28. Sharwood, S.: Australian bank stops handling cash at the counter in some branches. https://www.theregister.com/2023/04/04/australian_bank_no_cash_tellers/. Accessed 02 Sept 2023

29. Sienkiewicz, S.J.: Credit cards and payment efficiency. Federal Reserve Bank of Philla Payment Cards Center Discussion Paper (01–02) (2001)
30. Sun, W., Zhang, K., Chen, S.-K., Zhang, X., Liang, H.: Software as a service: an integration perspective. In: Krämer, B.J., Lin, K.-J., Narasimhan, P. (eds.) ICSOC 2007. LNCS, vol. 4749, pp. 558–569. Springer, Heidelberg (2007). https://doi.org/10.1007/978-3-540-74974-5_52
31. Tan, H., Chen, X.: The no surcharge rule and its welfare implication. Int. Rev. Econ. Finance **89**, 1369–1384 (2023)
32. Transport, Q.: Payment options for transport and motoring services. https://www.tmr.qld.gov.au/Help/Credit-card-surcharge. Accessed 02 Aug 2023
33. Tut, D.: Fintech and the COVID-19 pandemic: evidence from electronic payment systems. Emerg. Mark. Rev. **54**, 100999 (2023)
34. Verdier, M.: Interchange fees in payment card systems: a survey of the literature. J. Econ. Surv. **25**(2), 273–297 (2011)
35. VISA: Visa payWave. https://www.visa.com.au/pay-with-visa/featured-technologies/visa-paywave.html. Accessed 02 Aug 2023

Author Index

N. Dong et al. (Eds.): SDLT 2023, CCIS 1975, p. 147, 2024.
https://doi.org/10.1007/978-981-97-0006-6

Printed in the United States
by Baker & Taylor Publisher Services